MW00561814

The Laptop Repair Workbook

An Introduction to Troubleshooting and
Repairing Laptop Computers

Morris Rosenthal

Please Read

The author has done his best to provide accurate and up-to-date information in this book, but he cannot guarantee that the information is correct or will fit your particular situation. The book is provided with the understanding that the publisher and the author are not engaged in rendering professional or engineering services. If expert assistance is required, the services of a competent professional should be sought.

Flowcharts produced with Microsoft Visio Standard

Editor – Tracie Shea
Technical Editor – Chuck Berg
Copy Editor – Kira Taylor
Proofreader – Franklyn Dailey Jr.

Copyright 2008 by Morris Rosenthal

Published by Foner Books

www.fonerbooks.com

ISBN 978-0-9723801-5-7

TABLE OF CONTENTS

Before We Begin Troubleshooting

The author of this book is the proud owner of a 1986 Dodge Omni that was purchased new and has never been taken to a garage for repairs. But laptops aren't cars and they are rarely as cost effective to repair as desktop PC's. A twenty or forty year old car in good operating condition is just as serviceable as a new car and may even get better gas mileage. But a ten year old laptop isn't going to run the latest Microsoft operating system or even the previous version. Computers are no better than the software they can run. You're going to need an up-to-date operating system if you are a mainstream user who wants to run the same software you use in work or the current year tax program. A laptop computer that cost as much as a new small car in the 1980's isn't worth a gallon of gas today. Think of computers as software appliances. Unfortunately, laptop computers are among the shortest lived appliances found in the American household today.

If you make an appointment with a doctor for a health issue, the first thing you might expect to hear is, "So, what seems to be the problem today?" This is the most important part of the diagnostics process for a good physician, listening to the patient describe the symptoms and asking some follow-up questions to probe deeper. The patient who responds, "I don't know what's wrong with me" might get a blood test or a psychiatric battery but is unlikely to walk out of the office with a cure. When it comes to diagnosing your laptop problems, the laptop is the patient and you are the physician. The laptop usually can't describe its symptoms, so you have to be a keen observer of laptop behavior if you want to nail the problem your first time out.

Some health issues, like puncture wounds and broken limbs, manifest themselves in an obvious manner so there's no difficulty with the doctor or patient diagnosing the problem. The same is true if you've broken the hinges off your laptop, if the battery burst into flames or if you knocked your orange juice over the keyboard and it stopped working. The solutions are generally both obvious and expensive, and since laptops aren't family members, replacement is often the most sensible solution. But the majority of laptop symptoms, at least at first blush, may be attributed to any number of different problems. And, just as human beings have pre-conceptions and neuroses clouding the diagnostic picture, laptops have software issues that pose as hardware malfunctions. In extreme cases, laptop technicians will talk the owner into the "Nuke and Pave" approach, using the manufacturer supplied software to restore the laptop to its factory fresh condition to see if that solves the problem. Sometimes this makes more sense than letting a technician spend several hours (and several hundred dollars of your money) trying to solve a suspected software problem. But you can do this just as easily at home.

Information about
the book:

www.fonerbooks.com
/workbook.htm

This book can't make you into a professional computer technician. It will help you troubleshoot your laptop problem and take the most cost effective approach to repairing it, getting it repaired, or replacing it. But the troubleshooting process depends on your observations of the symptoms and your willingness to keep your mind open to solutions other than your first impression, or those suggested by friends who say they had "exactly the same problem." If the laptop is still usable but acts up, pay close attention to when and where it acts up, whether the problem always occurs after the laptop has been moved, or shut-down for the night, or running all day. Even the weather plays a part in troubleshooting some problems, so try to read through all of the general troubleshooting sections, just to get a feel for the things that go wrong with different components. If it doesn't make you into a laptop hypochondriac, it will make you a stronger diagnostician.

You may notice we don't talk about the razzle-dazzle technology of computer components in this book. The reason is simple. You can't upgrade or repair your laptop by using the latest technology available, nor can you save money by repairing it with older technology rescued from a random laptop at the recycling center. You have to use the exact parts your laptop was engineered to work with. Hard drives and memory are the only replaceable parts that are often compatible between models of a similar vintage. For some readers, the lack of an illustrated discussion on how hard drives store data bits will take some fun out of the book, but that knowledge can't help you when it comes to troubleshooting. There are plenty of books with beautiful color illustrations that try to explain basic computer technology, but they do so at the expense of helping you solve real laptop problems.

Two final notes about using this workbook. First, if your laptop is in warranty, it doesn't make any sense to take it apart in hopes of fixing something yourself. This book can still help you troubleshoot the problem to determine if it's a software setting or incorrect use, which may save you sending the laptop out for repair. Second, feel free to cut out the twelve flowcharts in the second half of the book and staple them together. This will save on page flipping as you read the expanded explanations of the decision symbols. It's a workbook, not English literature.

Laptop Basics

If you're already familiar with computer terminology, laptop components and values, you can skip to the general troubleshooting section. The discussion here will be strictly limited to describing the function of basic laptop components and the acronyms used to describe them. You don't need to remember what individual words the acronyms represent anymore than you need to remember that FBI stands for Federal Bureau of Investigation if they're knocking at your door. Acronyms are only a tool for describing certain computer components and functions, so think of them as labels and don't get caught up in the alphabet soup.

Operating System (OS)

We're confident that readers are familiar with the term operating system, but the acronym OS may only be widely recognized by Apple iBook and PowerBook users, since Apple operating systems have long been branded with "OS" and the version number. We always use "OS" on the flowcharts in order to fit operating system related decisions into the flowchart symbols, so it's the most critical acronym in this troubleshooting book. Also, when we refer to operating systems in this book, we refer to Microsoft Windows components and tools, since it's far and away the most widely used OS on laptops. There are excellent help groups online specific to Apple OS releases and Linux, especially the Ubuntu release which is gaining popularity as an alternative laptop operating system. The hardware troubleshooting procedures are as generic as we can make them in the absence of a "standard laptop," since no such thing exists.

Basic Input Output System (BIOS)

You may already be familiar with the separate roles played by hardware and software in computing. The hardware can be viewed as the body of the laptop, including the brain. The software can be viewed as the mind that controls the hardware in response to your requests. Sitting between the individual hardware components and the OS software that you use (most likely a version of Microsoft Windows) is a small chunk of hardware-specific software that allows the two to communicate. This software is known as the BIOS (Basic Input/Output System) and it is stored in nonvolatile memory on the main circuit board, or motherboard, of the laptop.

The BIOS is the first software loaded into regular memory (RAM) when the laptop is powered on. The BIOS contains sufficient instructions to operate the screen in a basic mode, to accept input from the keyboard, to read from the hard drive and the DVD/CD drive, and to detect attached network and USB devices. The latter is necessary because some laptops in corporate or government settings are configured to boot (to start loading the operating system) from a network or external drive for security reasons.

The memory chip on which the BIOS software is stored is a type of EEPROM (Electronically Erasable Programmable Read Only Memory) known as Flash Memory. Using software downloaded from the website of the laptop manufacturer to upgrade the BIOS to a new version is called "flashing." In many instances, if you call tech support with a problem, they'll ask a few questions and then suggest that you flash your BIOS with the latest version. Unfortunately, this standard procedure can turn your laptop into a useless paperweight if something goes wrong, like a power interruption or accidentally downloading the wrong BIOS for your model. The process isn't reversible without special equipment to reprogram the EEPROM. You only get the one chance.

We never recommend flashing a laptop BIOS unless you have specific information from web research that it is the exact and only cure to the problem you are trying to solve. It should never be necessary to flash the BIOS in order to recover some lost functionality. There are three common scenarios which may require you to flash the BIOS. The first scenario is if you are installing a specific software or operating system application that has a known problem with the original BIOS and for which a fix has been introduced. Laptop manufacturers often concentrate their efforts on getting Microsoft Windows right and only correct problems with Linux and other alternative operating systems at the BIOS level when reported by user groups. A new or upgraded version of Windows may also require a BIOS upgrade. The second scenario is an ACPI (Advanced Configuration and Power Interface) issue that may manifest in charging problems, fan management, or trouble with on/off, sleep or hibernation. Modern operating systems take charge of all of these functions from the BIOS soon after the laptop boots, but again, don't try flashing the BIOS when troubleshooting a power problem unless you have specific information that it must be the solution. The third scenario is if you choose to upgrade an internal hardware component with a part that wasn't supported by the original BIOS, such as a faster CPU or a Blu-Ray optical drive, you may find evidence that it will only work if you flash the BIOS with the latest version.

CMOS Setup

Another term that we're forced to use in this book is CMOS Setup. The CMOS acronym stands for Complementary Metal Oxide Semiconductor, the type of memory chip used to hold the user modifiable hardware settings. The CMOS Setup program is part of the BIOS and can be accessed before the operating system loads. Some manufacturers allow for CMOS settings to be altered through the operating system as well, through a hardware setup icon in Windows Control Panel, but the setting won't take effect until the next time the laptop is rebooted. After this brief description, we'll try not to mention CMOS Setup unless you need to access it for troubleshooting purposes.

It's entirely possible to purchase a laptop new and own it for years without ever knowing or caring that CMOS Setup exists. The most common reason the average user will ever have to enter CMOS Setup is to set a BIOS level password for the laptop, one that is required before the operating system will even try to boot. If your laptop comes equipped with a finger print scanner or other hardware based security, it's likely that the failsafe password is created and stored in CMOS Setup. Since the vast majority of laptops are sold with the operating system installed, the CMOS settings are preset to work with the operating system. However, if you wipe out the current operating system, or attempt to set up a dual boot system with Linux or another operating system version, you may have to change some CMOS settings. Many troubleshooting scenarios will require a CMOS Setup option that appears in the main menu under a title similar to "Restore BIOS Defaults" or "Restore Safe Settings". This option will restore all of the settings in CMOS Setup to the factory defaults, which can cure many problems if they've been corrupted or accidentally changed.

CMOS Setup is normally accessed before the operating system boots, using a key combination that is often displayed on the screen by the BIOS during the power on phase. Common access methods are hitting DEL key, ESC key or the F1 or F2 key immediately after you power on. Some laptops suppress the BIOS generated message in order to minimize user errors, but you can always go online and Google the right key combination if it's not in your manual. Note that the terms "BIOS" and "CMOS Setup" are often used interchangeably online when you're searching for the key combination.

Drivers and Device Manager

There are two types of drivers in laptops, hardware and software. The focus here will be on the software device drivers as the other type of drivers are board-level integrated circuits that aren't user replaceable if they fail. Software drivers, which we'll refer to as device drivers from here on, are the bits of programming that allow the operating system and other software applications to communicate with and control the hardware in your laptop. Since laptops are sold as whole functioning computers, rather than as expandable kits, all of the device drivers the laptop needs to function will be preinstalled. However, if you purchase an expansion card or add any external devices other than a few very standard components, such as a keyboard, mouse or memory stick, the laptop will require a device driver to work with it properly.

If the new device is widely used and has been around for a while, it's possible that the operating system will include a pre-loaded driver for the device, which it will find and install on its own when the device is connected. But in most cases, any device or peripherals you purchase, such as printers, cameras, USB speakers or broadband modems, will come with their own driver disc and specific instructions for how to install them. Frequently, the instructions will require that you install the software before hooking up the device for the first time. This is to make sure that your operating system doesn't try to install a seemingly compatible device driver for the hardware before the proper device driver is made available.

The drivers can be manually checked for problems and updated or disabled in the Device Manager view, which is found through Control Panel. The appearance of the Device Manager view and the way it reports potential problems varies between Windows versions, and in more recent versions it's a tab under the Hardware category behind the System icon in Control Panel. In all versions it will quickly give you three critical pieces of information about the status of your attached or installed devices. First, if it doesn't show up in Device Manager at all and no unidentified devices are shown, Windows doesn't know it's there, which means it's a hardware troubleshooting job. If the device doesn't work, but Device Manager shows it and indicates that it needs a driver, you haven't got the proper software driver installed. Finally, if it shows up with the right driver but Windows displays a specific error, like the hardware isn't responding, you need to troubleshoot that error.

Motherboard

Laptops are very close to being single board computers, where that single board is most commonly called the motherboard. Any additional circuit boards in the laptop that connect to the motherboard are known as daughter cards, so it's clear who won the computing gender wars. Unlike desktop PCs, where motherboards can be easily and inexpensively replaced in all but the most unfriendly systems, laptop motherboards are proprietary. The only replacement motherboard that will physically fit into your laptop is a motherboard of the same brand and model family.

If the motherboard fails and the laptop is out of warranty, it will rarely make sense to repair it. A new motherboard ordered from the manufacturer usually costs more than a new laptop purchased in chain store. If you're very happy with the laptop, except for the motherboard being dead, you might look for a used replacement part on eBay. If the failure is with a simple connector, like the power jack with its limited solder connections, it may make sense to repair the board yourself or to send it out. Just make sure you remove the hard drive before sending your laptop to some cheap power jack repair place you find online.

Central Processing Unit (CPU)

Surface mount vs socketed CPU

www.fonerbooks.com /laptop19.htm

The brain of any computer is the CPU (Central Processing Unit). This is a single, large silicon chip which is usually manufactured by Intel or AMD. It can be replaced as long as it is socketed, rather than soldered to the motherboard. Total CPU failures are relatively rare, but the CPU may misbehave or shut itself down if it gets too hot. It's fairly common for desktop PC hobbyists to upgrade their CPU with a faster model when the prices come down but it's rarely practical or possible with laptops. Unless the laptop motherboard was designed to support the faster CPU, it won't work at all. If you are able to find a faster CPU that will work in the laptop, it's unlikely to offer a performance difference that you can notice in normal usage.

Modern CPU speeds are measured in GHz (Gigahertz), or billions of cycles per second. If you own an older laptop, the CPU speed might be measured in hundreds of MHz (Megahertz), which expresses millions of cycles per second. CPU speeds used to increase rapidly from year to year and offer a reasonable estimate for system performance. Unfortunately, the CPU manufacturers hit the wall a couple years ago in terms of upping the clock speed, so performance gains are now achieved by cramming multiple brains into a single CPU. How much additional speed you see from employing multiple brains depends very much on the software you are using and the tasks you are working at. If your main applications are web surfing and e-mail, the speed and power of the CPU are nearly irrelevant. If you are editing video or recalculating spreadsheets with thousands of columns, CPU performance can turn a five minute rendering task into a two minute render, or a 20 second calculation into a 5 second calculation.

Your laptop may contain multiple heatsinks, which are finned metal structures that help conduct the heat away from hard working silicon components. The heatsinks installed on the CPU and the video processor are often active heat sinks, meaning that there's a little fan bolted right to the top of the heatsink to help cool it. This is a key reason to rethink upgrading your laptop CPU even if it turns out there's one available for the motherboard. The faster CPU will likely generate more heat, and the laptop may not be designed to cool it. If a heatsink fan fails or is unable to provide sufficient cooling, the laptop will display overheating symptoms, like random freezes or shutdowns.

Random Access Memory (RAM)

The memory in your laptop is, by definition, the RAM (Random Access Memory). It's worth making a point of this because even some long time computer users confuse memory with storage, which leads them to ask the wrong questions at stores and purchase hardware they don't need.   When computer professionals and salespeople talk about storage, they are talking about devices that save data when the power is turned off. This can include hard drives, magnetic tapes, optical discs such as CD, DVD and Blu-Ray, even the old floppy disks. What makes it more confusing is that the Flash memory technology mentioned in our brief BIOS discussion is a form of permanent storage used by digital cameras, cell phones, and portable USB storage devices. But the main memory in your laptop is the super fast RAM that forgets everything when the power is turned off.

Memory in modern laptops is measured in hundreds of megabytes (MB) or a couple gigabytes (GB). The standard Windows operating system can't work with more than 4.0 GB of RAM, and the minimum suggested for running Microsoft Vista is 1.0 GB, so the overall range today is extremely narrow and memory is getting cheaper all the time. In general, the only laptop upgrade we recommend is the memory, but only if you're starting from a low amount. Most laptop motherboards only have room for two RAM modules, the little circuit cards that carry the individual RAM chips. We could feed you a lot more

SODIMM RAM in laptop:

www.fonerbooks.com /laptop18.htm

acronyms referring to different types of module technologies and speeds, but all you need to know is that you can only install the RAM that is specifically supported by your motherboard.

Hard Drive

Inside a 2.5" hard drive:

www.fonerbooks.com /laptop17.htm

The primary storage device in your laptop is the hard drive. Modern hard drive capacities are measured in hundreds of gigabytes, though just a couple years ago, they were limited to tens of gigabytes. It's enough space unless you load up on video, audio or pictures. If you do run out of space, clean up your existing hard drive by copying most of the junk onto DVD's or an external hard drive. It will be much easier than to upgrade the existing hard drive to a higher capacity and reinstalling all the software. It's usually possible to upgrade the hard drive with a higher capacity model, but the only practical method is to use special software to image your existing hard drive onto the replacement drive in an external USB enclosure, and then swap the drives.

Solid-state hard drives are now available in some high-end laptops and will slowly trickle down into consumer models over the coming years. Since solid-state drives have no moving parts, they should prove more reliable, will be more tolerant of physical shocks, and will use less power. But no technology is perfect, and it's probable that solid-state drives will prove vulnerable to certain hardware failures, such as electrical shocks. Unlike standard hard drives, when a solid-state hard drive fails, it's unlikely any data recovery will be possible.

DVD/CD Burners

Everybody has long known DVD and CD discs from home entertainment, but it's only in the past couple years that DVD recorders became standard items in laptops. The DVD recorder software will come with an option for recording data, which is a great way to create permanent back-ups of your important files. Most laptops also ship with a utility that allows you to create emergency restore discs, if they don't provide you with a factory recovery disc. The restore discs are a set of DVD's that record a perfect image of the hard drive and allow you to restore the laptop to its factory fresh condition should the hard drive fail or the operating system get hopelessly corrupted by viruses and malware.

The majority of complaints about DVD recorders are about their playback, not the recording. Many users use the DVD exclusively for playing movies, but the evolving copy protection schemes and encoding used by the various movie studios complicates the issue. Sometimes, a laptop will be able to play old movies, but not new ones. Other times, only movies from a certain studio will fail. It's even possible for an automated software update to result in a loss of capability, where a movie that played yesterday won't play today.

Liquid Crystal Display (LCD)

The LCD (Liquid Crystal Display) was the display technology breakthrough that made laptop computers possible. Before LCDs, there were some portable computers known as "luggables" that employed a small tube display that took up half the room and power. LCD screens are lightweight, consume minimal power, and unlike the old-fashioned tube displays, are well suited to getting bounced around. The LCD panel itself acts as a sort of electronic color film, but the images it produces are nearly invisible to the eye. If you remember the old 35 mm slides that used to be popular in photography, you'll remember how hard it was to make out the picture without a slide projector or a light table.

Taking apart a laptop screen:

www.fonerbooks.com /laptop_4.htm

The light source that turns the LCD "film" into a bright display is called the "backlight." The current generation of laptops employ a special type of fluorescent light, a CCFL (Cold Cathode Fluorescent Lamp) tube, which provides a bright white light that is evenly distributed behind the LCD screen by reflective surfaces. The CCFL tubes are very thin and relatively long lived, but they require a special power source to light them. This power is provided by the inverter, a circuit that transforms the low voltage DC power your laptop runs on into a high voltage, high frequency electronic signal. Inverters are the Achilles heel of laptop display systems. If the LCD only displays the faintest of images, it means the backlight isn't lit. Inverter or wiring failure is more common than actual backlight burn-out.

Showing inverter and backlight

www.fonerbooks.com /laptop_5.htm

Laptop Batteries

It's worth mentioning battery technology in laptop basics just to point out that laptops contain more than one battery. The battery everybody knows is the main battery which is easily removed from the laptop, costs around $100 to replace, and can power the laptop for a few hours when fully charged. All laptops also contain a small battery, similar to the batteries that power wrist watches, to maintain the time, date and the CMOS Settings. In addition some laptop models employ a non-removable battery for backing up the contents of main memory when the laptop is switched into hibernation. Higher end laptop models with a hot-swap bay offer the option of a second main battery for extended operating life, at the expense of removing the DVD drive or second hard drive.

Universal Serial Bus (USB)

Many years ago, laptops and PCs sported special connection ports for printers and slower external devices like dial-up modems. These ports have long since been replaced by USB (Universal Serial Bus) ports. Most laptops feature at least two or three USB ports, and on newer laptops, these are all the high-speed USB 2.0 and soon to be 3.0 variety. The USB ports on your laptop are even more valuable than the USB ports on your PC because they save you from expensive and impractical repairs by serving as a bypass for failed laptop hardware. The only downside of replacing failed laptop components (such as the keyboard, touch pad, DVD, modem, network and sound adapters) with external USB devices is that they slowly turn your portable laptop into a stationary desktop. But when your laptop is a couple years old and you are faced with a multi-hundred dollar repair that you might not be up to doing yourself, the ability to plug in an inexpensive USB device is a lifesaver.

PC Cards

Unlike standard PCs, most laptops aren't designed to accept any internal expansion cards. Those laptops that do employ a mini-PCI slot are usually sold with that slot already filled by some standard option. With the advent of USB 2.0, this has become less important, but you may want to add functionality to your laptop that requires more power or speed than USB provides.

This option is available through the one or two external expansion slots on your laptop known by the unfortunate name "PC cards". The earlier version, which you may see in a hand-me-down laptop, were called PCMCIA cards, which is too long an acronym to break out here. OK, it stands for People Can't Memorize Computer Industry Acronyms. The current standard in most laptops is Type II PC Cards, and they are primarily used for plugging in cellular modems, which allow your laptop to communicate at a modest speed over the cellular phone network, for a steep price. The latest generation of laptop expansion cards are called "Express Cards" but they have seen limited adoption so far.

Wireless Technology

Since we just mentioned cellular modems, it's a good time to bring up the wireless technology, WiFi. WiFi networking for computers is distinct from the cellular phone network; WiFi and cellular simply refer to different wireless technologies. WiFi networking is strictly a short distance solution. Current standards support ranges from a few tens of feet up to a few hundreds of feet, depending on the generation of wireless equipment used. The most common WiFi implementation used in laptops today is the "G" standard, which is generally backwards compatible with the older "B" standard. That means a laptop with built-in B/G will be able to operate on either type of network. The most recent release to achieve popularity is the "N" standard, and the newest laptops and after-market adapters support wireless B/G/N. While "WiFi" and "wireless" may be used interchangeably by computer professionals, "wireless" is rarely used when referring to cellular communications.

Bluetooth

Bluetooth adds another communications dimension to laptops, though it's not commonly used for local connections despite its wide availability. Bluetooth is another wireless standard that offers simplicity combined with relatively low capacity. It's currently the favored technology for wirelessly connecting cameras, cell phones and headsets to laptops, but this could easily change if WiFi hardware becomes cheaper or Bluetooth hardware gets faster. In most applications, Bluetooth is a convenient way to eliminate a cord as opposed to the only way to get the job done. Most laptop users with built-in Bluetooth capability probably never use it, or even know that it's there.

What's My Laptop Worth?

When a laptop suffers a major failure, the first thing to do is estimate both a repair cost AND a replacement cost. We aren't fans of the disposable culture or the waste involved in replacing equipment that can be repaired, but we'd be doing you a disservice by ignoring the cost trade-off between repairing and replacing a laptop. When calculating the replacement cost, it should be based on the cost of a brand new laptop that meets your needs, not on some high-end model that has everything you could possibly dream of and only weighs three pounds. What you paid for your current laptop two or three years ago has no relationship to the value. You may have gotten a great deal, you may have been ripped off, but laptop technology has been advancing rapidly and prices have fallen dramatically, especially if you know how to shop.

You may save a lot of money by troubleshooting and repairing your own laptop, especially if the cost of having it repaired for you is so high that the only logical alternative would be to buy a replacement. Yet it turns out that you can usually find a new laptop that will suit most purposes for between $400 and $500 in the U.S., by shopping for new laptops that are nearing the end of their product cycle and thus have rebates. Not only will it come with the latest operating system installed, but the battery will be new and the unit will be covered by a manufacturer's warranty. The best comparison shopping source to locate laptop bargains at the major electronic chains is www.salescircular.com, which simply aggregates the Sunday newspaper specials with rebate information from the major electronics outlets in every state. We specified the U.S. above because laptops in many countries are subject to special duties or sold through exclusive distribution networks that double the price and greatly impact the repair/replace calculus.

In case you decide to go the route of buying a new laptop, don't buy with the intention of upgrading or the attractive price will dissolve like a desert mirage. Never buy the extended warranty from the store. While you'll occasionally run into somebody who bought the extended warranty and ended up with a lemon they had replaced, the stores sell these warranties because they are profitable for the stores, not for the consumers.

It's difficult for people to let go of their original purchase price as a starting point in assigning a value to their laptops. But new cars that famously lose a percentage of their value when you drive them off the lot don't age as quickly as laptops, and you can still drive a fifty year old car on the highway. You can't get on the Internet with a twenty year old laptop, and you need to be a little eccentric (and very patient) to do it with a ten year old model. The built-in wireless which allows you to access the Internet from public places or anywhere in your house with a wireless router has only been around for a few years, and the same is true for laptops capable of running Microsoft's Vista operating system.

Shopping For Used Laptops

Shopping for used items is a passion for some people, but if we could only give one word of advice about buying a used laptop, it would be "Don't." Fortunately, talk is cheap so we'll go on at length about when it does or doesn't make sense to buy second hand and how much to pay for different capacity models. But remember you can almost always find a new laptop for under $500 in the U.S. at a local big-box retailer. You'll get a brand new laptop with the latest Windows installed and enough memory to run it, a big hard drive, a combination DVD/CD recorder and player, built-in USB 2.0, WiFi, 56K modem and a wired network connection as well. The battery will be new, so you'll actually be able to work untethered for a few hours at a time, and you'll be able to expect two or three years of trouble free operation if you don't abuse it.

New laptop purchasers often have an old one to sell, so they're available everywhere from eBay to newspaper ads, company-to-employee sales to PC shops, and of course, Internet sites. The major used laptop sellers on the Internet are usually selling reconditioned or remanufactured units, where reconditioned basically means they turned it on and it worked and remanufactured means something was broken so they replaced it. The term "factory second" means it failed the final test at the factory, so instead of shipping it, they reworked it on the spot and didn't sell it as new. Sort of like buying scuffed shoes at a discount clothing outlet.

There are more brand name laptops than desktops sold these days, with some popular models being the Dell Latitude, Toshiba Satellite, Sony Vaio, HP Pavilion, Lenovo Thinkpad, Acer Aspire and Apple iBook. Most of these models have been around forever, which means you can't just buy a Satellite and assume that you're getting a recent Toshiba laptop. The Thinkpad, Sony Vaio and the Apple laptops probably hold their value a little better than the other brands, because they are rarely sold at deep discounts, even on closeout. However, there's no reason to pay for name recognition in a used laptop, and notebooks that have operated long enough to be sold used are well beyond any initial quality concerns.

Second hand laptop prices are often advertised as discounted from their list price. Their original list price! You couldn't find a laptop priced for less than a grand a few years ago. A company that bought a bunch of cheap laptops a few years back for a $1000 each and is now replacing them with new laptops will offer them to employees at 50% off. The employees believe it's a great bargain and pay $500 for obsolete junk with worn out batteries (with the software removed if the company is conscientious) when they could be buying a brand new laptop for the same price that's several generations better. The same thing happens with the used and reconditioned notebooks sold over the Internet or on eBay. The seller says, "List price $1,699" or "I paid $2,349" but they're talking about retail laptop prices without rebates that are two or three years old.

Look carefully at the capabilities of these notebooks. Their CPU speed probably doesn't meet the latest operating system requirements, they won't have much memory installed, nor a DVD recorder, and if they include wireless, it may be an external adapter. The battery will be on its last legs, and the screen will have dead pixels, and the USB ports will be the older 1.1 version. The keyboard and mouse pointer will be old and unresponsive. The model that "listed" at $1,699 will be promoted as a steal at $795, and the $2,349 laptop (with "$1,000 of software I added") will have a minimum bid of $1200. They may get it too, but not from you. You could be buying a new high-end laptop for that kind of money, with a new warranty, the latest legal software and all the bells and whistles.

Then, you finally find some cheap used laptop prices, between $200 and $400. Sounds a lot better on the face of it, but here's what we found doing a little Internet shopping today. The "Special" on one of the Internet's top sites was a 650 MHz HP notebook Pentium III with Windows 98. They were selling it for $429 before shipping and handling. That's eight year old technology! No wireless, an 18 GB hard drive (cheap new notebooks ship with 100 GB hard drives, five times the capacity), and while Windows 98 was a good release, Windows XP or Vista are required to install most new software. The same store offers a whole range of used laptop models for $299, all with tiny hard drives (6 GB), less than a fifteenth of what you'd get in a $500 new model), Windows 98, 128 MB of RAM and CPU speeds under 400 MHz!! These are typical prices for used notebooks, and you're paying 60% to 120% of the price of a new laptop for one that won't run software you need and can't be upgraded. All over the Internet you'll see second hand laptops with Pentium III CPU's selling for between $500 and $1000, advertised as bargains, it's just insane.

Price Range	Advice
$400 - $500	Buy a brand new laptop with factory and store rebates. Make sure you fill out the rebate paperwork correctly, stick with in-store rebates if possible.
$300 - $400	The only used laptop we would recommend buying in this range is a lightweight or desktop replacement model running Windows XP or Vista, with built-in wireless and a DVD recorder, and then only from somebody you know.
$200 - $300	If a friend or family member has a laptop less than one year old that they want to sell you because they've bought a better one, just make sure it suits your needs and check the battery life.
$100 - $200	You can gamble a little in this price range, meaning if you're buying a beater laptop to drag around, as long as it has wireless and works, you might get what you paid for.
$0 - $100	Before you accept a free laptop, understand that the local landfill will probably charge you $10 or $20 to dispose of it if you find it's not any use to you.

This value analysis ignores one major factor; the software and data on your hard drive. If you've installed software and no longer have the original installation discs, or programs that won't function under a new operating system, you may be willing to spend more on repairs. If you have data on the hard drive of a dead laptop you haven't backed up, treat that as a separate issue. If the hard drive is still alive, the data can be easily read off in another machine. Just remember these two things. First, your laptop is going to die or become obsolete sooner or later and probably sooner, so at some point you'll be throwing good money after bad. Second, one of the most common and cost effective laptop repairs is to replace a failed hard drive. Unfortunately, a failed hard drive means the loss of your programs and data unless you have back-ups.

Ironically, the most sensible purchase of a used laptop you can make is purchasing a broken one, providing it's the exact same model as yours and you need the good parts. For example, if your laptop experiences a motherboard failure, it's normally a death sentence since new motherboard prices are prohibitive. If you can find somebody selling the exact model on eBay with a dead hard drive and a cracked screen, needless to say, you'll get it cheap. Then you can move your hard drive and LCD to the replacement laptop, and you're back up and running, with parts to spare.

Shopping for New Laptops

Shopping for a laptop based on how much you can afford is a mistake that normally leads to spending too much. You need to determine what functionality you require before you start shopping for a new laptop. For some users, the style and the color of the laptop will be the deciding factor, and nothing we can write in this book is going to change your taste or priorities. But if your interest in purchasing a laptop is to acquire a tool for accomplishing certain tasks, we can probably save you some money.

We aren't going to refer to specific CPU brands and speeds, memory technologies, hard drive access times or the latest generation of anything. In the context of this book, we're assuming you're shopping as an alternative to gambling on an expensive repair that may not solve the problems with your current laptop. Getting you fixed up with your dream laptop isn't the point, we just want to make sure that if you do buy a new laptop, you buy one that will meet your needs for a couple years.

Laptop manufacturers design their different model lines to appeal to different markets, though the basic functionality of all the units when sitting on a desk and plugged into a power outlet is very similar. The processor speed and the hard drive capacity are far less important to the average user than the built-in options, such as digital film readers, a web cam, or extended life battery and hot-swap capability. Despite the best efforts of the manufacturers to segment the laptop market into distinct audiences with increasing price points, they do a fairly poor job at explaining the differences between their model lines. So your principal homework before you start shopping for a new laptop is to determine which of the following groups you fall into.

Basic Consumer Model

The least expensive laptops, the ones we keep referring to as being available new with or without rebates in the $400 to $500 range, are the basic consumer models. These laptops generally represent the state of the art - of the previous year – and are designed primarily for low manufacturing cost. Despite the less-than-exciting design goal, these laptops are still very capable and powerful machines because they are sold in a very competitive environment. They normally weigh in the five or six pound range, come standard with the latest Microsoft operating system, and are unfortunately loaded with "free" trial version software.

The basic consumer model laptop will run any standard software you buy. It simply won't run that software as fast as a model that's designed for high performance. The standard laptop will happily connect to the WiFi hotspot in your home or local café, and will offer high speed USB connectors for hooking up printers, scanners, cameras, etc. It will have a practical battery life of two or three hours, and a reasonably good LCD display. It probably won't have any advanced security features, such as a fingerprint scanner or face recognition, but these features are less practical than showy.

The Home Entertainment Laptop

Once the province of desktop PCs, laptops have pushed into the home entertainment market, especially with younger consumers who may move frequently and appreciate the all-in-one approach of having the screen, computer, DVD player and Internet connection all in one small package. Laptops designed for the home entertainment market tend to have faster CPUs and larger screens, employing the 16:9 letterbox format which is ideal for movie playback and some gaming applications. They may also feature brand-name video processors and better sound reproduction than standard consumer models. However, there's only so much you can get out of tiny laptop speakers and limited amplification, so most people using a laptop for home entertainment will purchase USB speakers. More serious gamers, at least for the near future, will stick with desktop PCs, as a high performance video adapter for gaming requires more power than an entire laptop, and costs more than a low-end model as well. Home entertainment laptops run from $600 to $1000.

Business Laptops and Tablets

Laptops targeted at business users are more likely to feature docking station connectors. Docking stations allow the laptop to be quickly installed in a base that ties it into all of the business systems in your office, such as the network, printers, a standard keyboard and mouse, all without fooling around with multiple USB connectors and networking cables. Docking stations may also offer a DVD recorder, or other devices missing from a super lightweight laptop. Business models are also more likely to support hot-swap bays for flexibility, so you can install a second hard drive in place of the DVD drive, or a second battery for that eight hour flight. They also tend to ship with less junky trial software, since corporate IT departments have less patience and more say in the matter than the average consumer.

A hybrid laptop/tablet design is becoming more popular with students and businessmen alike, although the original tablets were quite distinct from laptops in their design. The hybrid laptop/tablet employs a screen with a single hinge point in the middle that allows the touch screen capable LCD to be swiveled all the way around and laid back over the keyboard,

24

with the screen facing up. At this point, the laptop functions like a very capable tablet, and can be used for taking notes longhand, drawing, or stepping through checklists and forms with a stylus, a popular business application for field representatives. Prices for tablets and business laptops range from $700 to $1500.

Desktop Replacements

Laptop manufacturers struggle to draw a line between their home entertainment and desktop replacement lines, but that line is rapidly disappearing. The key design goal of desktop replacement laptops is to come as close as possible to the performance and capacities of desktop PCs without sacrificing portability. This results in heavier laptops that draw more power, have shorter battery lives, and often sport outrageously large screens. The assumption behind desktop replacements is that they will usually be placed on a reasonably sturdy desk or table, plugged into the wall, and stay in the same place most of the day. But, unlike desktop PCs, you can actually take these on the bus or the plane if you need to, and specially designed backpacks and rolling luggage are making this a more practical option. For the salesperson who travels by car and sets up shop in a motel room every night, it is the next best thing to bringing his entire office with him.

Desktop replacement users will often opt for a port replicator. A port replicator is the poor man's version of a docking station, and port replicators sold by the manufacturer often use the docking station connector. Aftermarket port replicators that use the PC card slot or USB port can't offer quite as much functionality, but they are portable between systems and may meet your needs better. Port replicators allow you to connect USB devices, a keyboard, mouse, wired network, etc, by plugging them into the port replicator rather than attaching four or five cables to the laptop. That way, when you want to take the laptop to the coffee shop, you only have to pull one connection, and you're on your way. Desktop replacements are priced in the $800 to $2000 range.

Lightweight Travel Laptops

Finally, we come to the luxury cars of the laptop world, the lightweight travel models. For starters, you can expect to pay between three and five times the cost of an entry level consumer laptop for a reduction of about 50% in weight. Lightweight laptops may weigh as much as four pounds, if they feature a full size keyboard, a reasonable size screen and a permanently installed DVD recorder. But as you move up in price and down in weight, the screens and keyboards become smaller, and the standard options you have come to expect in even the cheapest laptops begin to drop away. The first feature to go in lightweight laptops is normally the DVD drive. Rather than featuring a hot swap bay for flexible configuration, the lightweight laptops are more likely to offer an extended life battery as an option, one that adds size and weight to the laptop.

You won't find a lot of choice for true travel notebooks when you check your local big box retailer, though they may have a small Sony Vaio for around $2,000 and some version of a light Toshiba. Shopping for serious lightweight notebooks is best done on the manufacturer websites. After you zero in on the exact model that suits your needs, you can try shopping other websites on price, but there's usually not much variation in the high end models. Sony, Dell and Lenovo (Thinkpad) are the lightweight or sub-notebook leaders, but Toshiba, HP and Acer also sell models that come close to the four pound limit, and don't leave you stuck carrying around an external DVD drive. Lightweight laptops can cost anywhere from $1000 to $3000.

Laptop Upgrades

First, let us reiterate that you should never buy a used laptop with the intention of upgrading it. If you've owned a laptop since buying it new or if it was given to you as a hand-me-down, an upgrade may be worth looking at if you need a little more functionality.

The easiest and most effective upgrade most laptop owners can make is upgrading the RAM. A ancient second hand notebook with 32MB of RAM will see a major performance increase (especially when you open multiple windows) if you upgrade it to 64MB, and an old notebook with 64 MB will run "like new" if you add 128MB for 192MB total. Newer laptops with 256 MB or 512 MB installed can often be upgraded to 1 GB, but if your plan is to install Microsoft Vista, make sure the rest of the hardware, especially the CPU, is up to speed.

Laptop RAM is usually upgraded by removing an access panel on the bottom of the notebook that's secured by a single screw, and snapping the new module into place. However, upgrade capacity is normally limited to a single module unless you remove the factory installed RAM, and the size and technology of that memory module is fixed in advance by the laptop manufacturer. Consult your owner's manual or visit the memory guide at crucial.com before attempting to upgrade. The trick is to first make sure your laptop doesn't already have the maximum amount of RAM installed, and to buy the right module. Also, some laptops don't feature easy access to the RAM slots, and you'll have to remove the keyboard or open up the body.

Now comes the bad news. The RAM is the only internal laptop component that can be easily upgraded. The problem is three-fold. First, laptops are highly proprietary, and an upgrade part like a DVD burner that will fit the physical form, provide the right connector and be supported by the laptop BIOS may not exist. In some instances, you may be able to use the outer plastic bezel and metal frame from the original CD/DVD-ROM to match a new recorder to the body of the notebook, but it still has to be a supported model. Second, these parts are so much more expensive than desktop components that it's not funny. Your best bet is to buy "pulls," components scavenged from broken or discarded units, but even these aren't cheap. Your current laptop BIOS may not support the new CD or DVD drive, or even a larger capacity hard drive. Never fool around with flashing the laptop BIOS unless you are absolutely desperate, because if it goes wrong, you'll be left with a brick. Third, while you can generally install a larger hard drive, it probably won't be any faster and transferring all of your software is quite a job and rarely a simple task.

You can't upgrade the motherboard in your laptop. In most cases, you can't even replace it cost effectively if it fails. The same goes for the LCD screen, though you can hook up to an external monitor if your screen is failing and you aren't ready to replace it. You may be able to upgrade the CPU if you're desperate for performance, but it's better to start by installing the maximum amount of RAM and to clean up your operating system. The reason laptop manufacturers design some motherboards with a CPU socket rather than soldering the CPU

Illustrated RAM upgrade:

www.fonerbooks.com /laptop_2.htm

to the motherboard is it allows them to use the same motherboard in a wide range of model-price points, with the CPU speed being the main differentiating factor. By designing the laptop with a replaceable CPU, they can avoid committing to manufacturing fixed quantities of each model before they see how sales go, and keep their options open should CPU prices fall dramatically. But unless your laptop was one of the lowest performance models in the family, it's unlikely that upgrading to the fastest CPU available will make much difference. It's also a more delicate job than upgrading the memory, and may require a dreaded BIOS upgrade as well.

So, have we eliminated any hope of recording CDs or increasing the storage capacity of your old laptop? Absolutely not. Laptops are designed to work with peripherals, and as long as you have a USB 2.0 or even an older USB 1.1 port, you'll have no trouble finding inexpensive external drives that will also be portable to any other computer you own or may purchase in the future. For moving data between computers or storing a few gigabytes of data, USB JumpDrives are a great solution. You can carry a JumpDrive on your key chain (and many are designed for just that), and read the data on almost any computer in the world. You can also connect to a router for high speed internet access through your USB or the network port. Another handy notebook upgrade is an external mouse and keyboard. A simple USB splitter for less than $10 will provide both ports in one convenient rat tail, especially handy if your notebook has only a single PS/2 port for a keyboard or a proprietary keyboard port.

If you're feeling depressed about the limited upgrade options for your laptop versus a desktop PC, look on the bright side. Laptops are "green" computers, in the sense that they are designed to use the minimum amount of materials (for reasons of weight) and to run on batteries. The requirement for all laptops to run on batteries makes them far more power efficient than desktop PC's, where manufacturers compete on performance. Most laptops run on appreciably less electricity than a 60 watt light bulb, while the power demands of desktop PC's can be five to ten times as much. Of course manufacturers of expensive laptops want to compete on performance as well, and in some cases they might actually dip into the battery reserves for peak power demand even when the laptop is plugged in.

Things That Go Wrong With Laptops

The main selling point of laptops is that they are portable and can operate on batteries. Not surprisingly, two of the main drawbacks of laptops are that they are portable and can operate on batteries. Portability leads to a whole series of problems that you don't normally encounter with desktop computers. About the worst of these problems is that laptops are easily stolen or lost, simply by forgetting them in funky places, like on top of the car or on the bus or train. Beyond losing the whole laptop, portability introduces the problem of getting banged around and stepped on. You won't encounter too many desktop computers with cracked LCD screens, but people often treat closed laptops like a plank of wood, which they aren't. Stacking things on top of laptops, especially in overhead baggage compartments, can result in enough point pressure on the lid to crack the screen. Component or board level damage is also possible when sufficient violence is done to a laptop.

For most electronic products, high reliability is achieved by reducing the number of moving parts. Unfortunately, laptop designs universally feature a hinged screen that is opened and closed each time the laptop is moved somewhere. While the engineers have gotten very good at designing the hinges and the cables that bring signal and power to the LCD screen and backlight in the lid, they are still moving parts. Intermittent problems with notebook screens that seem to come and go at random after you move the laptop are usually related to the opening and the closing of the lid. One time the wire twists the right way, next time the wire twists the wrong way. The wiring bundles are no fun to fix, and doing any repair job on a laptop that requires working with the hinges can lead to wires getting broken or shorted. All this means that if you aren't going to be carrying your computer from place to place, you're better off buying a desktop.

Batteries, which make laptops such popular café and classroom accessories, are another Achilles heel that desktops do without. Battery technology has advanced tremendously in the last 20 years, but the same basic problems still plague all high power battery devices. Battery packs achieve a high enough voltage to operate a notebook computer by including multiple battery cells connected in series. This makes it very difficult for the computer to fully comprehend the state of discharge of the battery pack as a whole. Additionally, with some technologies, user behavior makes a huge difference in how long the battery will remain viable. The most recent battery technology to achieve wide acceptance is Lithium-Ion. These battery packs are the least demanding in terms user lifecycle management, but they have issues of their own, like limited shelf life and occasionally bursting into flames.

Another generally unremarked flaw of laptops is the moral hazard. The convenience and portability of laptops promotes reckless behavior on the part of their owners. Who hasn't been guilty of working on shaky tables in cafes while traveling, with a tall Pilsner glass or a paper cup of coffee just inches from the keyboard? If somebody bumps into the table or elbows over the glass, it could be curtains for the computer. Eating and drinking over a desktop computer normally only puts the keyboard at risk, a $10 replacement part. Eating and drinking around a laptop puts the whole unit at risk should liquid find its way past the keyboard membrane and cause a short circuit. A sticky desktop keyboard is easy to clean or replace, while a sticky laptop keyboard is a nightmare to clean, and will cost around $80 to replace if you do the job yourself, and as much as $250 if you pay somebody else.

If you do spill something on your laptop, the best bet is to hold in the power button (and your breath) for three or five very long seconds to turn it off. The normal human reaction of pulling the plug after spilling a liquid on electronics doesn't accomplish much when the battery is installed. After it shuts down, unplug it if it's plugged in and sop up as much of the liquid as possible with a paper towel. Once it's turned off, if you have to turn the laptop upside down to remove the battery, sopping up most of the liquid before it gets past the keyboard membrane is probably a better choice. In any case, when you've cleaned it up as good as you can, remove the battery and let the laptop dry out overnight. If it was anything worse than a little splash of water or coffee on the keyboard, remove the keyboard to check for any signs of wetness underneath before attempting to power it up again. You should find some well illustrated disassembly instructions for your model online.

Leaving laptops in cars is another killer. You don't want to leave your laptop in a hot car anymore than you want to leave your children or your dog. Well, there are laws against leaving children and dogs in cars, and unless you're a cloning advocate, they can't be backed up. Backing up your laptop is your only defense against all of the awful things that await it in the world. The only critical component in your laptop when it comes to preserving your data, your programs, your favorite websites and e-mail addresses, is the hard drive. A nasty jolt at the wrong moment, a bad power surge, too much heat or an overturned cup of coffee can all lead to a hard drive's premature demise. There are services that can recover most of the data from hard drives that aren't too badly damaged for a cost between a few hundred and a few thousand dollars, but making it happen in a hurry costs extra.

Backing Up

Backing up your important data on a DVD on a regular basis means you can walk into any electronics store, walk out with a cheap new notebook, and be up and running again within a couple hours. If you run a business, are in the process of writing a novel, or have other information that you need to back up every time you use the computer, there are two more choices. One is to buy a cheap JumpDrive (a USB memory stick with four or eight GB of storage) and copy your most frequently used data onto it whenever you've made substantial additions. The trick, of course, is to keep the JumpDrive in your pocket when you aren't using it and not the USB port, where it could walk off with the whole laptop. The other option is to sign up with a remote backup service that uses the Internet combined with software on your computer to incrementally backup every change you make. Of course, it means another password to remember and another monthly bill. The poor man's version of online backup is to simply create a free account at Yahoo!, Google Gmail or MSN Hotmail, and e-mail yourself attachments on a regular basis.

Moving beyond the hardware, the most frequently encountered laptop problems are due to software. This situation isn't unique to laptops, as a profusion of software is equally as bad for desktop PCs. A huge number of laptops are replaced because they've slowed down so much they're barely usable. Laptops don't get slower with age, the clock that ticks along a billion or so times a second to drive the digital brain of the laptop never changes speed. Laptops get slower when they are overloaded with software or attacked by malicious programs. The new and often unwanted software gives the laptop more and more to do until it can barely finish anything.

If your laptop came with a factory rescue DVD or CD, and it hasn't gotten scratched up, you can always run the recovery software to restore the laptop to the exact state it was in when it was new out of the box. Of course, it didn't have any of your data or software on it when it was new out of the box, so you better have a perfect backup before taking what technicians call the "nuke and pave" approach.

Malware And Protection

When presented with a laptop that takes forever to boot and runs incredibly slow for a period of time afterwards, the main culprit you'll encounter is improperly configured anti-virus software. Anti-virus software is a necessity for protecting Windows based computers that are connected to the Internet. The problem comes about when the anti-virus software is configured (intentionally or unintentionally) to run a full scan every time the computer is booted. A full scan means that the anti-virus software ignores the fact that it's already checked every file on your hard drive and checks them all again. This can take anywhere from fifteen minutes to a couple hours, depending on how big your hard drive is and the speed of your laptop. During this time, the anti-virus software is not only eating up processing power, it's also continually accessing the hard drive, and the little hard drive activity LED will be lit almost continually. The operating system is happy to let you try to do other things while all of this is going on, but the performance will be so bad that you'll be sure that you have a virus when what you really have is too much cure. You'll also encounter laptop computers that have multiple copies of anti-virus software from different vendors trying to run at the same time, or one after another. There's such a thing as too much caution.

The best way to meet your need for anti-virus software, anti-spyware software, anti-adware software and firewall, is to buy an all-in-one suite. Kaspersky, AVG and Avast are some of the more reliable and friendly suites, but you aren't likely to see them preinstalled on a new laptop. Technology columnists and PC magazines like to produce articles comparing and rating the various suites, and often give you the impression that not buying the top rated package is like leaving your doors wide open. As long as your suite does daily updates of the virus database, you should be fine unless you spend all of your time exploring the dark side of the Internet. The big brand-name security suites used at your office or your bank (and which may be pre-installed in a trial version on your laptop) are usually a lousy choice for home use. These suites are often resource hogs, require a bit of specialized knowledge to configure well, and can be extremely unfriendly to honest software applications you install.

When the user of an unprotected laptop ventures into a bad neighborhood, often after being misled by a search engine result or a link on a social networking site, the result can be some form of browser hijack. Your browser has probably been hijacked if as soon as you connect to the Internet, ads start popping up in your browser, or your home page has changed to some innocuous looking directory site you've never heard of. In milder cases, downloading and running a security suite after the fact may fix the problem, though you might have to do the download on another computer and copy the installation files to CD or a memory stick for the stricken laptop. That's only if you're lucky though. Security software is best suited to keep malicious programs off your computer. Once they get in, removal can be a long manual job, with you or the technician constantly going back to Google and searching for the next piece of the puzzle. It can take a computer professional six or seven hours to clean up a laptop after a particularly nasty browser hijack and trojan installation. Even then the solution depends heavily on somebody else having figured out the cure and sharing it online. Since an ethical computer technician doesn't want to charge you $300 to $500 in time for cleaning up a malware infestation, the total reinstall, or nuke-and-pave option, is often taken.

Aside from malicious software, laptops face the usual run of software related problems. There's accidental deletion of program files and icons, registry corruption, poorly written programs not playing nicely together and over-full hard drives. While you could spend the rest of your life typing and not put a dent in your hard drive capacity, pictures and video from digital cameras or music and movies downloaded over a high speed Internet connection can eat through space at an amazing rate. Your laptop counts on having some hard drive space available at all times to use as a scratch pad while managing the data in memory. If you don't leave enough free space open, you'll start getting crashes and file corruption.

Perhaps the most annoying problem faced by the buyer of a new laptop is all the undesirable free trial software the laptop manufacturer has been paid to include. After booting up a new laptop and registering the operating system, the first thing to do is to get rid of all of the trial software, especially the anti-virus, and replace it with a product of your choosing. This can take a few hours, as many new laptops need an hour of clucking away to themselves to unpack all of the software baggage pre-installed on the hard drive in compressed form. The length of this process depends on the manufacturer, and they usually include a slip of paper in the packing box letting you know that the laptop will need to spend a little time alone after it's powered on.

Basic Repair Techniques

Before we move on to troubleshooting laptop hardware, it's a good idea to cover some basic techniques you can use to increase the odds of actually fixing the problem, rather than making it worse. Here's the #1 favor you can do yourself. Before taking apart your laptop, search online for an illustrated repair procedure for your exact model family. Your best friend in searching for online repair guides is Google, but be prepared to spend a good hour or so looking for a well illustrated page. You'll need one that shows the procedure you need to carry out, or at least how to get the body open without breaking anything.

Laptops usually ship with a User's Manual in PDF format on the hard drive, which can be read on screen or printed through Adobe's free Acrobat Reader. But the user's manual is normally limited to some simple upgrades or component replacements and illustrated with a limited number of line drawings. The actual repair manual is sometimes included with the pre-installed documentation. If not, you can often find it on the laptop manufacturer's website or through Google. For recent models, you should try the manufacturer's website first, but don't be surprised if you find the repair manual poorly illustrated.

Getting Set Up

The next tip is to create your own illustrated guide as you go along! You don't have to do any writing or plan on publishing it, but a digital camera can provide invaluable documentation and help in finding your way back should the repair prove more complicated than you hoped. It's easy to forget whether a cable ran to the right or left of a drive, or above or under another cable. Yet these details are planned out by the engineers and may be important to promote air flow or prevent abrasion. Unless you're doing a hardware hack, the laptop should go back together exactly the same way as it came apart, and a couple dozen photos from your digital camera can make all the difference. Digital photos are free, so don't skimp.

A large, flat workspace with good lighting is also a key ingredient to a successful repair. You can't expect to fix your laptop working on your lap, unless you're doing something really simple, like replacing the RAM. Ideally, you should create a workspace where you'll be able to leave the disassembled laptop for as long as the job takes. Keep in mind that the troubleshooting process doesn't always identify the right problem, or the only failure. You don't want to have to put the whole laptop together again just because you're waiting for a part to show up, or a longer block of open time to work on it. Although laptops are pretty rugged when screwed together, many of the components are quite delicate when they are removed from the laptop, or left hanging from a connector. Moving a laptop around in a disassembled state is always a bad idea, even if you put it in a box.

Screwdrivers And Screws

Screwdrivers are the only tools you need to do the majority of laptop repairs, but you'll often need more than one. Most laptops are put together with Phillips head screws, but these are the small electronics sizes. The Phillips screwdrivers most people have around the house are #2 or larger. The largest size that you might use on a laptop is the smaller #1, and you'll almost always need at least one of the #0 or #00 sizes. All three of these, the #1, #0, and #00 can be found in any decent electrical precision screwdriver set. In a pinch, you can also use jeweler's screwdrivers, but jeweler's screwdrivers have very slim handles that make it difficult to generate the torque needed to break some screws free. Laptop screws are installed with a little thread adhesive to prevent vibration from loosening them up. Most people doing home repairs don't bother using new adhesive when reinstalling screws, though you can purchase it at your local hardware store.

Tips for laptop
disassembly:

www.fonerbooks.com
/laptop13.htm

Don't fool around with trying to remove screws with a cheap all purpose tool that comes with dozens of replaceable screwdriver bits. Not only will the bits have trouble fitting in some of the recessed holes, they tend to flake apart and they often strip the screw or Torx head as they fail. A single stripped screw head can stop you dead in your tracks on a laptop repair job, so it's important to use a quality screwdriver that's the right size for the screw and fits easily into any recessed holes.

A bigger problem than removing the screws is keeping track of them. It's important to know which holes screws came out of when the screws are different lengths. If you put a screw that's too long in the wrong hole, it may punch through and damage something. Even if they don't do damage, screws that are too long won't hold the laptop closed properly, and screws that are too short won't hold anything. Sometimes the holes are labeled with numbers molded into the plastic, where the numbers might refer to the screw length, or they might refer to the screws that must be removed for a specific procedure. If you're going to count on those numbers, label the first screw you remove for each number and make sure all the following screws match it.

Otherwise, you can take several approaches to tracking screws, all of which can have their drawbacks. The first is to label each screw hole with a pencil or a bit of masking tape and a pen as you remove each screw. If you've never worked on a laptop before, you can make a line that's the length of the screw for a label. If you've worked on enough laptops to be familiar with screw lengths, you can use letter labeling, like "L" for long and "S" for short. Unfortunately, you can end up with one of those nightmare laptops that use six or seven screw lengths just to hold the body together, leaving you with extended labels like "LL" for longer long, and "MS" for medium short.

Some people try taping the screws right next to the holes, but this gets awkward if you take a bunch of screws out of the bottom and then have to work with the laptop upside-up. The tape can come loose and the laptop won't sit level and will feel unstable when you're working on the top. Another approach is to make a map of the screw holes on a piece of paper, either by drawing it or by poking holes in the paper where the screws go. Then you can tape the screws to the map as you remove them. If you have a really large work area and aren't worried about disruptions from kids or pets, you can just lay the screws out on the table in the pattern you remove them, but they are prone to rolling out of position if you give the table a bump.

Static Electricity

Static electricity discharge is always a worry when working with laptops, but you don't have to rush out and buy an anti-static mat if you're not going to be doing repairs on a regular basis. The main thing is to be sensible and not to work on the laptop in an area where you get a static shock every time you touch the doorknob. You should avoid activities that create static build-up on your body, like removing clothing in the middle of the job because you're getting frustrated and overheated, pacing back and forth on the rug, or stroking the cat in an attempt to calm yourself down. Ground yourself before digging into the laptop by touching a grounded appliance or the screw in the center of a grounded outlet. You can purchase a static bracelet on a tether for a few dollars online or at your local electronics store, but if you aren't used to working with one, you can end up catching the cord on something and knocking parts off the table or into the open laptop body.

Disconnecting The Power

Before you start any laptop repair, you should unplug the laptop and remove the main battery. If your laptop is equipped with a secondary battery in a hot swap bay, remove that as well. The main danger of working with the battery installed is that the laptop may be inadvertently powered on, which would lead to all sorts of component damage if it happened at the wrong moment. Once the laptop is disassembled, you may need power to continue with the troubleshooting, for example, if you're trying a spare backlight. At that point, it's often better to use the AC power than the battery power because the AC power adapter can be quickly disconnected if there's a problem. If you power up with the battery, there's no quick way to power back down again in an emergency.

Windows Device Manager

Windows Device manager has been using the same symbols to display device problems from early versions right up through Vista. A problem is expressed by any extra symbol, like a "!" or a "?" appearing next to a device. Double click on the problem device(s) or else click on the little "+" to the left of any questionable devices to get the expanded view. When you double click on any specific piece of hardware in the expanded view, you can select the Resources tab, where there's a little box in the lower half that reports on conflicting devices. Write down any information in the box, rather than trusting it to memory.

A red "X" means that the device has been disabled, but is still eating hardware resources and may cause conflicts with other installed devices. This information appears on the "General" tab of Device Manager, the first screen that comes up when you double click on a specific device or right click and choose "Properties." At the bottom of the screen there are two check boxes or a pull down menu under the heading "Device Usage." If the "Disable in this hardware profile" box is checked or selected, uncheck it or select "Enable" and then reboot.

A black "!" next to a device means Device Manager sees a problem, but the device may actually work. It could be caused by a conflict or a version problem with the driver, so try updating the driver from the manufacturer's website. A blue "i" doesn't indicate a problem as much as a warning that the device's resources have been set manually. This could be the result of your having cleared up a conflict by manually forcing different resources on a device. A green "?" means that a compatible device driver has been installed. The driver is the first thing to check if you're having any problem with a device, and running a compatible driver rather than an exact match from the manufacturer is often the fault. Device Manager also includes an interactive troubleshooting wizard that's worth a try.

The main Microsoft Knowledge Base article on Device Manager codes at press time:

http://support.microsoft.com/kb/125174

Searching for Answers

Internet search is the single most important tool at the disposal of technicians and home users alike these days. Whether you use Google or favor another search engine, a half hour of serious searching and reading can save you hundreds of dollars and many hours of frustration. Most readers will have quite a bit of experience with search by this point, but we're going to suggest a simple model that may increase your efficiency when searching on laptop errors or troubleshooting questions.

Let's say you power on your laptop and get the error:

```
Pxe-E61: Media test failure, check cable
```

The plain reading of this error is that there's a boot problem because the BIOS can't read the boot drive, and is reporting a test failure. While the connector may really be the problem, it's also quite possible that the hard drive electronics are failing or that it's not spinning up. Before you tear out your hard drive and put it in a USB enclosure to test on another computer or try to recover data, it's a good idea to search the Internet for reports of the same error in identical circumstances, to narrow down the possibilities.

When you go to search, the critical part of the error message is not the text, it's the code at the beginning, "Pxe-E61". In order to limit the search results to a reasonable number, combine the error code with some information about your model, or the circumstances surrounding your failure. For example, you might Google:

```
pxe-e61 acer aspire
```

or

pxe-e61 overheated

or even

pxe-61 spilled drink

The next step is to read the short descriptions Google presents with search results (ignore the advertisements at the top and the side of the screen unless you are searching for parts to buy). Pay special attention to the bottom line of each search result, which shows the website URL. The results you want to try first are those from the laptop manufacturer or discussion forums, including sites like: forums.cnet.com, daniweb.com, geekstogo.com, forums.techguy.org, asklaptopfreak.com, etc. Results from blog hosting sites are often pure advertising come-ons, populated with text scraped or stolen from discussion sites.

The next step is to quickly skim down the page to see if the problem being discussed is identical or at least very closely related to your own. However interesting the thread might be, and many encompass tragic human interest, you can't afford to spend ten minutes reading every page that comes up or you'll fritter away hours or days without finding the information you need. Do not try following links on the site in hopes they'll get you closer to your solution. A large number of the links are just advertising or spam, and even the honest links are far less likely than Google to get you where you need to go. So if the page isn't what you need, hit the back button, and try the next likely result in Google. If the back button doesn't work (some sites disable it to capture you), just type the Google address back into your browser bar.

You should be able to go through the first couple pages of results in a couple minutes if you only visit the sites most likely to offer real help. If you don't have a good answer to your problem at this point, rather than going to the fourth page of results, or the fortieth, it makes much more sense to rephrase your search. The general rule, if you are getting thousands or tens of thousands of potential results when you do a search, is to narrow down your criteria by adding more key words. So you might now search on:

pxe-e61 acer aspire overheated

or

pxe-e61 overheated acer spilled drink

It's OK if you get zero results, you've only wasted two seconds. But don't start out with super specific searches or you'll end up limiting the search engine's ability to show "quality" results, in favor of showing results that simply match all the key words. There's a lot of automated spam on the web created by programs that scrape text from different pages and string it together to fool the search engines into believing it's valid. Super specific searches may end up excluding the most useful results that have good discussions of the problem, but don't appear because they use slightly different wording.

Another source for illustrated laptop repair guides is authority sites. In web parlance, authority sites are those that collect links to web pages on a specific subject, and organize them in such a way that you can quickly find a link to the information you are looking for, if it exists. Many of the web pages listed on authority sites were created by non-professionals using a digital camera to document their journey into laptop repair. The reigning champion of authority sites for photo illustrated laptop repair guides is:

http://www.repair4laptop.org

Troubleshooting Power Problems

Because laptops are designed to be portable and function on battery power, they are engineered to run on the DC (Direct Current) power that batteries provide. But all of the power distribution networks in the modern world utilize AC (Alternating Current) because it's a more efficient and economical way to move electricity long distances. This means that laptops are shipped with an AC adapter that plugs into a regular outlet and converts that AC power into the proper DC voltage for the laptop. Most modern AC adapters for laptops can function on a power grid ranging from 100 to 240 volts AC. You should take a look at the label on the AC adapter, often called a "brick" before you go traveling around the world. All that's needed to plug a variable AC adapter into a different power grid is a new end for the plug, purchased at a local hardware store for around a dollar.

If your laptop doesn't turn on when you hit the power button, the power system is a logical place to begin the troubleshooting process. The laptop power system can be viewed as three separate parts: The A/C adapter that gets plugged into a power outlet on one end and into the laptop on the other end, the laptop motherboard or power regulation daughter card that monitors and distributes power to the laptop components, and the battery. The vast majority of laptops manufactured these days can operate without the battery installed. In some cases, the manufacturers will suggest that you remove the battery and store it somewhere cool if using the laptop in one location for extended periods of time, as in weeks or months. In all instances, it pays to read the owner's manual on how to best extend the battery life for the particular model.

One of the oddities about troubleshooting laptop power failure as opposed to PC power failure is that the battery gives the laptop an independent power system for as long as the charge lasts. If the PC in your home is plugged into a bad power outlet or its power strip is accidentally switched off you'll quickly figure out why. But if the power strip gets turned off while you are operating your laptop, or a breaker trips, or the local power grid suffers a brown out, you might not even notice until the battery runs down. That's why it's important to not jump to conclusions about laptop battery failures, and to try charging the

Power adapter connectors:

www.fonerbooks.com /laptop16.htm

43

battery under different conditions before giving up and buying a new one. Just because the battery didn't charge while the laptop was plugged in doesn't mean the battery is bad. The power to the AC adapter may have been interrupted, the AC adapter or cable to the laptop may have failed, the connector tip may have been partially plugged into the laptop, or the battery may have become partially unseated. There could also be something wrong with the laptop charging circuitry or software. Running out and buying a new battery before investigating all the possibilities will often mean a $100 or $150 mistake.

New laptops should have a status LED in a visible location on the front or keyboard surface of the laptop that tells you when the power input is good. However, that doesn't help you determine where the failure is if the LED doesn't light, or isn't lit steadily. A simple DC voltage meter can be used to confirm that the AC adapter is putting out the correct voltage, though it will usually read a little high since there's no load on the output. A harried technician may stick the DC connector on his tongue as a quick test to see if it's live, but you can't taste the difference between 12.5 volts and 18.5 volts, and you probably shouldn't try. Another crude check is whether or not the AC adapter gets warm while it's plugged into the laptop and a live power outlet. It shouldn't get hot, just warm to the touch if the battery is charging or the laptop is operating. Some AC adapters are equipped with a status LED right on the brick that tells you when the AC adapter believes it's functioning properly. Don't forget to make sure that the cord from the wall outlet to the AC adapter is firmly plugged into the brick.

Electronic devices often produce high frequency buzzes and whistles under regular operating conditions. Some people can hear these sounds, especially young folks and women, while older men tend to have very limited high frequency hearing. A high frequency whistling sound may indicate a capacitor in the AC power adapter is beginning to fail, but it will often whistle while it works for years to come. You don't have to replace the AC power adapter just because you can hear it, unless it gets worse and worse over time or it gives you a headache. Because AC adapters employ switching mode technology, they are more likely to make noise when the battery is fully charged and the laptop is turned off. AC adapter bricks are usually glued shut and aren't designed for consumer repairs, so unless you have solid electronic troubleshooting skills and a source for parts, it's a question of living with it or replacing it outright.

The most common laptop power failure is centered on the junction between the connector on the end of the AC adapter cord (the DC output) and the receptacle in the laptop. This one inch length of wire and connectors costs pennies at the wholesale level but leads to large numbers of laptops requiring expensive repairs or being junked. Often the copper wires inside the cord become frayed or broken right where they enter the connector on the end of the AC adapter cord. Sometimes you can struggle along for weeks or months by working on a flat surface and getting the cord into exactly the right orientation so that the wires maintain contact, but it's not a smart way to go. The wires (a number of very thin conductors twisted into a heavier cable) are sized for the amount of power the laptop requires. As thin wires break and lose contact, all of the power must flow through the remaining conductors, leading to overheating, which can cause damage or be a safety hazard. It's an easy enough fix, so don't ignore it.

Starting with the AC adapter plugged into the wall and unplugged from the laptop, there are number of clues to look for when plugging it into the laptop. First, if it sparks, unplug it and check for a short circuit with a multi-meter. No resistance (or less than a few Ohms) between the conductors of the DC connector on the laptop means there's a short circuit inside, which calls for taking the whole laptop apart. You normally can't get both multi-meter probes into the connector when the laptop is assembled, so measure between the positive input and a ground point of any exposed metal around the USB ports or other motherboard connected ports. The positive DC voltage input is usually the center pin of the barrel connector but you can determine this by measuring the voltage on the AC adapter to see if the outer or inner connector is positive. Often, short circuits will have caused visible damage, like melted or burnt chips or components on the motherboard. Other times, the short will be in one of the attached daughter boards or drives, so the standard procedure if you can't see the damage is to strip the laptop down to nothing except the motherboard, keep checking with the meter, and see if the short goes away. If it doesn't the short is on the motherboard, and if it's not obvious, the only fix is to replace the motherboard.

Replacing an AC Adapter connector:

www.fonerbooks.com /laptop_7.htm

Multimeter tests for voltage and shorts:

www.fonerbooks.com /laptop11.htm

If wiggling the cord causes the power status LED on the laptop to blink, the problem is in either the cord or the connector. Fortunately, all you need to repair the connector on the AC adapter cord is a new connector and basic soldering skills, or you can bring it to an electronics shop for a cheap repair but get the price before agreeing. Some laptops use a highly proprietary connector for which you can't easily find a replacement, in which case your best option is to find a failed AC adapter for your laptop model, cut the end off (with plenty of slack) and splice it onto your cable. But most barrel connectors are easy to come by and your local Radio Shack often has them in stock. Just bring your laptop along to make sure you get the right size. If you work on irregular surfaces (like a lap) and allow the cord to dangle, the wires may break just inside the connector due to pulling, despite the fact that the factory connector is encapsulated in molded plastic. You can carefully pick apart the molded plastic with a razor knife to temporarily fix a connection if you're desperate, but it's smarter to replace the connector end as soon as you determine it is causing intermittent power failures.

The real killer is when the connector inside the laptop fails. Sometimes the center pin of the connector breaks off, sometimes the solder joints on the main board fail, sometimes there's a break between the connector contacts and the motherboard contacts. In all these instances, you or the technician has to gain clear access to the main board in the laptop to make the repair. Even with clear disassembly instructions, it's a big job to attempt on your own and requires decent soldering skills. It might be worth the effort if your only cost effective alternative is replacing the laptop outright. The replacement connector usually retails for less than $10 (and wholesales for pennies), but the repair charge can be several hundred dollars for some models if you take it to a local shop.

Within the laptop itself, most components receive power by way of direct connection to the motherboard or through very short cables. In this way, laptops are less complicated than PCs, where the drives and some power hungry video cards are connected directly to the power supply by long cables with multiple connectors. Because of this, power failure to the hard drive or DVD player in your laptop is rare, and in most cases would be corrected by reseating the drive in the connector. But power failures can occur if the main board is damaged when the laptop is dropped or a foreign substance (like beer) is introduced. However, the laptop screen, its supporting hardware and any special features such as a web cam incorporated in the lid, are powered by cables running through the laptop hinge. When troubleshooting possible power failure to the components in the laptop lid, you have to eliminate cable failure in the hinge or at the cable connectors as a cause.

Troubleshooting Battery Problems

Laptop battery technology has come a long way from the early NiCad packs that had to be carefully managed. Otherwise their charge capacity would rapidly diminish to the point where an hour of unplugged operation was a fond memory. Some manufacturers did a better job managing NiCad battery life than others, but the only reason for nostalgia about those times was that the battery packs could often be rebuilt by the ambitious do-it-yourselfer. NiCad technology was largely replaced by NiMH (Nickel Metal Hydride) batteries in laptops, which have excellent charging and discharging characteristics as single cells, but which also proved to be tricky to recharge in a battery pack and required some management on the part of the laptop user for maximum life. Some technologists insist that NiMH batteries don't suffer from the same memory effects as NiCad, but nobody argues about their weight, both types of batteries being heavy.

Inside an old style battery:

www.fonerbooks.com laptop_3.htm

Most recent laptops are equipped with Lithium Ion (Li-ion) batteries, which are much lighter and don't require any special behavior on the part of the laptop user. However, they have a higher internal resistance which makes them prone to overheating at a high rate of discharge, so they have to be equipped with more sophisticated monitoring circuitry. There have also been a series of manufacturing problems with these Li-ion batteries that have led to recalls due to fire risk. One other negative characteristic of Li-ion batteries is they lose capacity, whether you use them or not, at a rate of 15% or 20% per year. However, since most laptops are a three or four years item at best, you should get through the life of your laptop with the original battery unless you go through a complete charge and discharge cycle several times a week. If you are having problems with a Li-ion battery, the first step is always to check on the manufacturer website to see if it has been recalled.

Li-ion batteries are "smart" batteries, and contain circuitry that helps to prevent them from overheating and catching fire. The chemistry of Li-ion batteries causes their internal resistance to rise with age and the number of charging cycles. In some instances, your battery may stop accepting a charge prematurely because an integrated "fuel gauge" shows that the cycle life has been reached. You can find hacks on the web for resetting the fuel gauge on some batteries, but we don't advise doing so. While the battery may work fine afterwards for an additional period of time, it may also overheat and damage the laptop or cause a fire.

If your laptop has two different size batteries, a main battery and another in a hot swappable bay, don't try to do any troubleshooting with both batteries installed. Troubleshoot your problem with the main battery first, and worry about the secondary battery once you achieve normal operation. If the bays and batteries are identical, you're in luck, because you can use process of elimination to determine if either one of the batteries or one of the bays is faulty. If you work at a company that has purchased a number of identical laptops, or if a family member or friend bought the same laptop as you, the simple way to diagnose whether the problem is with the battery or the laptop is to trade batteries for a day.

When laptop owners call tech support to report that their battery isn't charging or the life doesn't seem to be what it should, tech support will often tell them to download the latest BIOS. While it's marginally possible that the laptop shipped with a BIOS that has been improved in regards to battery management, the BIOS upgrade process, called flashing, is not reversible without special equipment. In other words, if something goes wrong, instead of having a laptop with a battery charging problem you'll have a collection of perfectly good laptop parts that won't do anything. Flashing the BIOS is a last resort we only recommend if you find references on the Internet that it fixed an identical charging problem for somebody else with your exact model. You can select the CMOS Setup option to "Reset BIOS Defaults" without much risk, which will repair any inadvertent changes that may have been made to CMOS settings.

The first step in troubleshooting battery life or charging problems is to check your owner's manual or the manufacturer's website for how to interpret the status LEDs on the laptop or the battery itself. Some batteries come equipped with built-in LEDs and a button you can press that will roughly display the battery charge by the number of LEDs lit, or show an error state, usually indicating that the battery needs to be replaced. On other models, the LEDs on the laptop will change color or blink when there's a charging problem. In either case the operating manual for the laptop or a search of the manufacturer's web site should tell you exactly what the LEDs are indicating. They won't be right 100% of the time, since batteries are tricky beasts, but you aren't taking a big gamble if you trust them.

If the LEDs indicate that the battery is being continually charged, yet the battery only lasts a short period of time, there's a good chance the battery is worn out or defective. Before giving up, perform one last test to determine if the operating system software is interfering with charging. Let the battery charge overnight with the AC adapter plugged in and the laptop turned off. If the battery won't take a charge with the laptop turned off, you can try powering on, entering CMOS Setup, and letting it sit and charge on the Setup screen for a few hours.

Even if the battery is healthy and the laptop charging system is working properly, the battery lifetime will be variable with how hard you work it. If you're in the habit of turning the screen brightness all the way up, playing a CD through USB speakers, and choosing the highest performance battery management profile, the battery will run down much quicker than otherwise. Newer laptops offer a number of predefined battery management profiles in the operating system, normally accessible through the little battery icon in the system tray, and your choice of options has a significant impact on the battery life. The ambient room temperature and the temperature of the laptop (if you've left it in a hot car in the summer or a cold car in the winter) will affect the battery life as well.

Over the years, some manufacturers have provided software to recondition batteries for certain laptop models. While software might be necessary to reset an erroneous charge count on a "smart" battery, it's a rare situation that an Internet search should quickly turn up something if it's required for your model. Other laptops include a special reconditioning option you can select in CMOS Setup. The built-in reconditioning software is simply a way to run the battery down to true empty, before recharging, which shouldn't be necessary for Li-ion batteries.

If you do purchase a new battery and the seller offers to take your old battery in exchange, go ahead and send it after you confirm that the new battery indeed solves the problem. Otherwise, you'll be stuck disposing of it at your local recycling facility, which may charge a few dollars to take it. Batteries are little chemical factories with all sorts of heavy metals and exotic compounds, so you don't want to throw them out with your kitchen trash, and it's probably illegal to do so where you live.

Laptop Video Troubleshooting

Backlight tube:

www.fonerbooks.com
/laptop_6.htm

We suggested in the introduction to laptop hardware that you think of the LCD as an electronic version of color film. The LCD acts like a film that passes different wavelengths (colors) of light depending on whether or not the liquid crystals are twisted this way or that, so a bright light source is needed to bring the display to life. The light source, located behind the LCD screen, is called the backlight. The vast majority of laptops manufactured today utilize a Cold Cathode Fluorescent Lamp (CCFL). This form of fluorescent light source has several advantages for use as a backlight, including low power consumption, long life and uniform lighting from a small form factor. The CCFL lamp used in laptops isn't much thicker than a boiled piece of spaghetti and is covered in a plastic sleeve that helps diffuse the light evenly over the length of the tube. The back of the laptop lid is also lined with a highly reflective surface, such as aluminum foil, to push all the light possible out through the LCD.

The one drawback with all fluorescent lights, as opposed to the cheap incandescent light bulbs most people still choose for home lighting, is that the fluorescent bulbs need a specially conditioned power source to fire up the plasma and cause the lamp to fluoresce. The voltage and frequency vary with the particular lamp used, but the range for backlights is around 400 to 800 Volts at a frequency between 30 to 70 KHz. The laptop component that supplies this lamp power is known as an inverter, a widely used term for devices that transform low voltage DC into higher voltage AC. The inverter for your laptop is one of the easier parts to replace, a small circuit board that usually costs between $20 and $80.

Inverter board:

www.fonerbooks.com /laptop_8.htm

Now, that was a lot of techno-babble to squeeze into two short paragraphs, and by no means is it a complete discussion of LCD technology. The important thing to come away with is the understanding that your laptop display consists of three basic pieces: the LCD screen that acts like a piece of electronic color film, the backlight which lights up the LCD from behind so you can see it, and the inverter that powers the backlight.

Assuming that the video processor on the motherboard is working properly and sending the LCD instructions as to which colors to allow through in which screen points (pixels), the most common failure for laptop displays is a dead or intermittent inverter. When you can only see a very, very faint image of your operating system desktop on the screen, it means that the video system is working, but the LCD isn't getting any backlighting. The usual culprit is the inverter, especially if you didn't note any strange tinting to the laptop display in recent operation, but it's not easy for the do-it-yourselfer to determine with 100% accuracy whether the failure is the CCFL lamp or the inverter. Some laptops, especially older models, have a brightness dial on the side of the lid, so make sure you don't have a laptop where the backlight can be manually turned off before continuing.

Backlight tests:

www.fonerbooks.com /laptop14.htm

The traditional method used by technicians to test inverters is to connect it to a known good backlight of the proper type. Since buying a spare CCFL tube for your laptop kind of defeats the whole point of testing the inverter, people without access to spare laptop parts will sometimes use a cheap CCFL tube from a PC modding kit, which can cost as little as $3 by mail order. While the test may not hurt the inverter, there's no guarantee that a negative result (cheap tube doesn't light) really means the inverter is dead, because the two may just be very poorly matched for each other. If you have access to a good quality RMS multi-meter through friends or work, one that can measure frequency to 50 MHz or 100 MHz, you should be able to get a reading on a functioning inverter without even taking the lid apart. The inverter is normally located below the LCD in models with narrow borders, or to the side if there's an inch or

Noninvasive
inverter test:

www.fonerbooks.com
/test.htm

so of plastic bezel on each side of the LCD. By scanning with the multi-meter probes over the plastic along the edge of the screen, you should pick up a strong signal somewhere between 30 KHz and 70 KHz if the inverter is live (note that a meter with a 50 KHz range will probably work well above that range). If you can't pick up the signal but want to be sure, remove the plastic bezel from around the screen and measure right on the two insulated wires leading to the backlight. If the inverter is functioning, the meter will pick up the signal right through the insulation, since the inverter is putting out a low radio frequency signal.

An important step in troubleshooting a laptop display problem is to plug in an external monitor. All standard laptops come equipped with a video connector that will drive an external LCD monitor, or even an old CRT. Sometimes you have to tell the laptop to switch the picture to the external screen, which is done through a keyboard combination on most models. Other laptops will detect on power up if an external monitor is connected and shift the display on their own. Look for the extra little symbols on your keyboard keys, which are selected when you depress the Fn (Function) key. You should find one that looks like a little laptop alongside a monitor, or something similar. Holding down the Fn key and hitting the key with the little monitor/laptop picture will either toggle the display to the external monitor immediately, or bring up a number of choices on screen if it's live. These may include choosing to display on the laptop only, the external monitor only, to display the same screen on both or to assign a primary and secondary display.

Some display problems aren't difficult to troubleshoot at all. If you notice an inky stain slowly spreading across your LCD over days or weeks that you can't wipe off, the LCD itself is failing. Dead and stuck pixels often appear on LCDs over time causing point failures in the display. There's nothing you can do to fix them, so just tolerate them if possible. If the laptop is fairly new, the LCD may be under warranty and the manufacturer normally has a specification for how many dead pixels a LCD can accumulate before they have to repair it. Other physical problems that may require LCD replacement are cracks and chips on the surface. Horizontal or vertical lines or swathes of either a single color or dead pixels usually mean the LCD will have to be replaced. This can be caused by the contacts on the

LCD carrying the pixel addressing information coming loose or the electronics controlling those lines failing.

Common sense plays a big part in troubleshooting laptop problems, especially when it comes to screens. For example, there are a whole variety of screen problems that come and go when you move the lid a little, from a stuttering back light to a missing color. In most cases, this indicates that the wire bundle running through the hinge has been compromised. Some wire has frayed apart and is making intermittent contact with itself or the lid movement is causing the wire bundle to pull on one of the video connectors. If there's a position in which the screen works properly and you don't have to close the lid to carry it around the house, you've found a temporary fix. If the problem has been getting worse with time, and it's harder and harder to find an angle for the screen in which everything works right, take that into account when it fails completely. In other words, if you've experienced a gradual failure that indicates the wiring in the hinge or a terminating connector is failing, that's the first place to look when you only get a faint image on the LCD. Without those early indications, it would be logical to suspect the backlight or inverter first, but common sense should tell you that the wiring and connectors are the place to start in this case.

There are also all sorts of problems with the display that can occur due to software settings. For example, an accidental (or intentional) keyboard combination can cause the display to start showing everything sideways! Other times, laptops with multiple users in families, especially where children are involved, will have the basic screen settings accidentally changed so that a blurry partial image is displayed. Although it can be tough to navigate through the screen settings in this condition, rest assured that it is just a software setting and not a reason to bring the laptop to a repair shop or call for in home service. Keep in mind that many electronic chains have a minimum charge for troubleshooting, and this can be over $100. Don't resort to using the emergency boot disc and restoring the laptop to factory fresh condition to fix this type of display problem. While the restore will likely resolve the display problem, it will also wipe out all of your data and any software you've installed on the laptop. Instead, try resetting the screen resolution and colors (accessed by right clicking in a open area of the Windows desktop and choosing "Properties" and

"Settings" from the resulting pop-up) to the highest color quality and the highest screen resolution, with the needle pushed all the way to the right. If you absolutely can't navigate because the image is so distorted, shut down and connect an external monitor, which should be capable of correctly displaying a wider range of screen settings, enabling you to change your settings there.

The most difficult type of display failure to troubleshoot is when nothing at all appears on either the laptop screen or an external monitor. How are you to know if the problem is really a video failure, and not a more fundamental failure with the power or motherboard? The main indicators in these cases are the sound, and the hard drive LED on the laptop case. If the laptop sounds just like it always does for a minute or two after being turned on, it means it's going ahead and booting the operating system, but the video processor or part of the motherboard circuit for video output has failed. If the laptop just sits there and beeps when you turn it on, or if you hear the fan but not the hard drive chuckling with its active LED flashing away, it means the laptop isn't getting as far as trying to boot the operating system. While this could be due to any number of hardware problems, the most common and easiest to troubleshoot or repair is RAM failure. If your laptop has two RAM modules installed, try booting with just one and then the other in the primary slot. If your laptop only has one RAM module, you might consider buying one online for $20 or $30, from a site with a good memory selector, like Crucial.com.

Laptop screens get very dirty, with fingerprint oil, dust, smoke, etc, and some people actually clean them from time to time. You should always turn off the laptop before cleaning the screen, and when the only culprit is dust, a soft tissue or lint free cloth can be used to gently wipe the screen without any cleaning products. The next step, for more stubborn obstructions, is to damp the cloth or tissue with a little water. If there's something stuck to the screen that the damp wipe won't remove without scrubbing, you can visit your local office supply store and buy a mild cleaner designed for LCDs. In no case do you want to spray anything on the screen as laptops and liquids make for bad bedfellows. If somebody insists to you that LCD's can be cleaned just like a mirror because they are made of glass, they are only half right, and it's the wrong half. The reason some delicacy is required is that there is a filter coating on the outside of the LCD, a kind of soft plastic, and your typical glass cleaner may degrade or discolor the coating.

Troubleshooting Laptop Overheating

Overheating is the primary reason for a laptop to work for a while when plugged into the wall, and then to freeze up or shut down on its own. There are two kinds of overheating involved, the first is component specific and the second is related to the overall temperature inside the laptop. Individual components, such as the CPU or video processor may simply get hotter faster than they should due to a manufacturing flaw or installation issue and we'll talk about these issues in the section about troubleshooting motherboards, CPUs and RAM. In this discussion, we're going to restrict ourselves to problems caused by the whole laptop getting too hot.

Overheating usually takes place in the body of the laptop, although it is also possible for the LCD electronics or the inverter in the lid to be adversely affected in a high temperature environment. Engineers employ a number of strategies to prevent all of the heat generating components crammed into laptop body from generating so much heat that they damage themselves. The most important strategy is limiting the amount of heat produced in the first place. That may sound like the ultimate design goal, but laptop manufacturers also have to compete with each other on performance, and higher performance components usually mean more heat generated. The main culprits in the heat generation cycle are the two large processors, the CPU and the video processor. Intel and AMD both manufacture special versions of CPUs for laptops, which run at lower power levels (producing less heat) when they aren't fully employed. Temperature management in laptops goes hand-in-hand with battery life management, since less power consumed means less heat produced, and a longer battery life.

Increased fan noise may be your first indication that your laptop is running on the hot side. It can be extremely irritating to work on a laptop with a loud fan that frequently cycles on and stays on for extended periods. A well designed laptop with good power management should be almost silent in normal usage, with the exhaust fan becoming audible only during periods of intensive computation. Fan speed is also controllable, so a well designed laptop will run the fan just fast enough to keep the temperature in the ideal operating range. However, some manufacturers go overboard on packing in high performance components to create a power laptop in the "desktop replacement" style, and these monsters tend to run hot even when they are in new condition. Go online and read some customer reviews of your laptop when you first suspect overheating. If the reviews include a common thread, like "the left side of the keyboard becomes too hot to type after fifteen minutes," it means your laptop was poorly engineered.

It's easy to find aftermarket products that are sold for the purpose of cooling down hot laptops. These range from passive devices that are intended to lift the laptop off the desk and provide for better air circulation, to stands with multiple fans powered from the laptop's USB port. These powered cooling devices might not hurt much while the laptop is plugged in with the AC adapter, but they don't make any sense when you are running on battery since drawing power from the battery increases its internal heat generation. But if you expect a positive contribution from a powered cooling device, find one that has its own power supply.

The most important thing you can do to prevent your laptop from overheating is to operate it in the proper environment. For starters, it should be placed on a hard, flat surface, with no obstructions within a couple inches of the sides and back. The flat surface can be at an angle, some laptops run cooler if the back is higher than the front as this increases passive air circulation. If you're going to use your laptop on your lap or some other soft surface, like a bed, find a board or some other flat, heat-resistant object on which you can place the laptop. If you're using the laptop for a short time on a non-ideal surface, like your lap, take a look at the bottom to see where the vents are and don't block them. And remember, if your legs are getting too hot for comfort, the laptop isn't very happy either.

Laptops are dependent on the surrounding air for cooling, so if you run a laptop in an environment that's too hot, it will overheat no matter what other precautions you take. The maximum operating temperature for most laptops is in the range of the 85° to 95° Fahrenheit (30° to 35° Celsius). You should check your operating manual to make sure, but generally speaking, laptops have a much smaller operating range, cool or hot, than people. That doesn't mean the laptop will immediately shut down or refuse to work if you take it up to the attic on a summer day, but heat is a merciless killer of electronic devices. Operating the laptop in a high temperature environment can lead to errors or data loss and shorten its life. By the same token, you can't let the laptop reach a high temperature while turned off by leaving it in a hot car or on a radiator, and then expect it to cool itself off when you take it somewhere nice and turn it on. Better to let the laptop cool down before powering it on.

Cleaning the laptop may solve your overheating problem if it's filled up with lint or if it has accumulated a blanket of insulating dust on its heatsinks, which are the metal finned structures placed on hot components to increase the surface area that can be cooled by air. Unfortunately, unless you partially disassemble the laptop, your cleaning efforts will be limited to blowing compressed air through the vents, which can also have negative consequences. You must use canned compressed air sold specially for cleaning electronics, as other compressed air sources may contain too much moisture and bits of foreign matter. You should also follow the instructions, especially if they warn you not to use the can upside-down, which may expel propellant. On the whole, if you're going to try to clean out a laptop that's experiencing overheating problems, you're probably better off finding detailed disassembly instruction on the web and carefully removing the keyboard or getting the top half off so you can see what you are doing. As tempted as you may be to use a vacuum, don't, unless you have access to a special static free electronics vacuum.

Cleaning laptop fan:

www.fonerbooks.com /lap_fan.htm

Troubleshooting Laptop Hard Drives

Hard drives were named for the rigid magnetic coated discs that replaced tapes and floppy discs for permanent storage in early computers, but the name is also fitting as they are the hardest working component in the computer. The rigid disc platters spin at thousands of revolutions per minute, while a magnetic read/write head floats over the surfaces, moving rapidly in and out on a precision positioned arm without touching the platters. This "flying height" clearance of a few millionths of an inch must be maintained even while the laptop is being jounced around in an airplane or a car. To put it in perspective, it's like trying to drive a car at high speed while keeping the wheels about a ten thousandth of an inch from the curb. But it works most of the time because the disc platter is smooth as glass and the shape of the read/write head is an airfoil that is lifted by breeze created by the rapidly spinning disc. Hard drives aren't sealed against the outside world, but the air exchange is through a very fine filter.

On very rare occasions, something goes wrong and the head touches the platter surface in a data area. This can occur if the laptop gets a jolt while the drive is working, if there is a manufacturing flaw in the head or actuator arm that eventually impairs their structural integrity, or if the hard drive is operated outside its design parameters, like at excessive temperatures or altitudes. The catastrophic result of the head touching the platter is known as a "head crash" and it's the worst hard failure can happen to your hard drive. Because the magnetic coating on the platter will be scraped off or destroyed where the head contacts it, the data will be unrecoverable by any means. In the aftermath of less catastrophic hard drive failures, such as the drive electronics or the data interface, you can send the drive to a specialist recovery company and pay some hundreds or thousands of dollars to get your data read off and returned to you on DVDs.

Hard drive test and data recovery with USB cage:

www.fonerbooks.com /laptop10.htm

Most replacement hard drives for laptops sell for under $100, but the ease of replacement varies with the laptop model and manufacturer. Many modern laptops do give you easy access to the hard drive by way of a small panel on the bottom of the laptop or through a drive bay on the side, so that the mechanical part of the job only takes a few minutes. But other models require you to open the laptop up by removing the keyboard or taking the whole body apart, so it's a good idea to check your user's manual or investigate your laptop's construction on the web before you order a new drive. It's always a good investment to pick up an external 2.5" USB hard drive enclosure for $10 or $15 so you can test your existing hard drive on some other computer and make sure it's faulty. Otherwise, you might spend a lot for data recovery, or decide you can live without any data that wasn't backed-up and buy a replacement laptop, without ever realizing that the drive wasn't the problem.

Troubleshooting software problems is far more complicated than troubleshooting hardware problems, yet most software problems get laid at the foot of the hard drive simply because that's where all of the software is stored. Many people assume that there's some fault with the hard drive when the drive activity light stays lit almost continuously and the laptop slows to a bare crawl, but that's the fault of the software, not the hard drive. Along with its duty providing high speed permanent storage for all of your programs and data, the hard drive gets co-opted by the operating system to serve as temporary storage, or virtual memory. When there isn't enough room in memory (RAM) to hold all of the programs and data the laptop is currently working on, that information is moved to virtual memory on the hard drive. If you don't have enough RAM installed in your laptop or if you are running multiple "memory hog" programs at the same time, the result will be a hard drive that gets beat on continually and can't ever catch up.

Another software issue that leads to an overworked hard drive is the installation of background programs that load automatically at boot and eat into your computing resources. The most common problem is improperly configured virus software that insists on running a full scan of every file on the hard drive whenever Windows is restarted. This can lead to the whole system crawling along for a half hour every time you reboot, with the hard drive working furiously away all the while. A different performance problem may manifest itself if you are participating in a file sharing network for music or videos or a shared telephony network. Aside from the fact that you may be putting your privacy at risk, you are opening the door to this external network to utilize resources on your computer, which can slow you down when you don't even realize you're sharing.

Easy type hard
drive replacement:

www.fonerbooks.com
/laptop_1.htm

As time goes on and you add new software for your digital camera, printer, scanner, etc, the boot time will get longer and longer and the overall performance will decline as well. Anytime a new software installation gives you the opportunity to add that software to your start-up programs, just say no. It's easier to start a program when you need it with the click of a mouse than to sit through an extra minute of boot time and the overall degraded performance that comes of having that software always loaded in memory.

Malware, from viruses to adware and spyware, can destroy your laptop's performance, compromise your security, and pollute your operating system so badly that simply wiping the hard drive and starting over again starts to look like a reasonable alternative. The only right way to deal with malware is to keep it off your laptop from the start. For Windows based systems, this means running a protective software suite, including anti-virus software, anti-ad software, anti-spyware software and a firewall. Some of these components are built-into recent Windows versions, but it's better on the whole to replace them with an all-in-one package that updates daily. If you have enough patience and access to the Internet, you can fix most malware problems after the fact. But this involves doing extensive research online and manually eradicating, one-by-one, the nasty programs that your belated installation of a protective suite can't cure.

Some laptops are shipped with a recovery DVD that will restore your laptop hard drive (and its operating system) to factory fresh condition. While this means losing any software you've installed and any data you haven't backed up, it's sometimes the most cost effective choice you can make. If you can't solve a malware problem yourself, it's likely that a computer shop will charge you hundreds of dollars to do so, whether successful or not. Frequently the store will point out on accepting the laptop that they are "not responsible for user data" and after seeing how bad the problem is, will do the factory restore themselves and you'll pay through the nose for having all of your data wiped out. Mail-in repair depots working under warranty are notorious for wiping out hard drives to "cure" problems, so it's always best to back up your data before letting anybody work on your laptop.

Laptops that don't ship with a recovery DVD provide software, and usually a desktop icon as well, for creating a DVD recovery set. You should do this soon after you purchase the laptop, carefully label the DVDs and store them in a safe place away from the laptop. The recovery set will normally consist of two DVDs, which is unfortunate, since much of that capacity goes to backing up all the unwanted trial programs the manufacturer has included on your new laptop.

Involved hard
drive replacement:

www.fonerbooks.com
/laptop_9.htm

Troubleshooting Wireless Connectivity

Laptops are one of the few computing devices to undergo a revolutionary change years after becoming mainstream. Originally, the main selling point of laptops was that they were mobile and could work on battery without a power outlet. Today, more and more people are inclined to think of laptops as Internet access appliances, since there are so many public places you can go with a wireless laptop and hop onto the Internet for free. Initially, wireless networking adapters for laptops were add-on options, first PCMCIA cards and later USB adapters. These days, all of the new laptops have built-in wireless adapters, and some are even moving in the direction of built-in cellular network modems.

People new to wireless computing often confuse WiFi technology with cellular phone technology. The wireless capability built-into laptops is known as WiFi, and is defined by the IEEE standard for networking, (802.11b/g/n and sometimes y), where "b" is an older, slower standard, and "g" is the most widely used. Faster and more powerful versions, "n" and "y" have been defined for some time but were only implemented in laptop hardware very recently. WiFi technology relies on low power transceivers built-into both the laptop and the modem/router that brings high speed Internet into your home or workplace. WiFi may also be transmitted through stand-alone routers or repeaters (access points) that are hard wired to a high speed network. The range of the current WiFi networks is very low, on the order 100ft (30m) within a structure, depending on the construction, and not more than a few hundred feet (100m) in the open air. Within that working range, the quality of the signal will drop off rapidly, leading to slower operation and lost connections.

The wireless adapters in laptops draw a couple watts of power that could be saved if you aren't on the web, and may also allow others to access your laptop if it's set up improperly. This has led most manufacturers to provide an external switch to disable the WiFi functionality. Not surprisingly, the first problem most new laptop owners encounter with trying to connect to a wireless network is that their WiFi has inadvertently been switched off. The next most common problem is that the signal strength is too weak to hold a connection. This can be extremely confusing if the network is working fine for a person sitting at the next table, but that laptop might have a more sensitive receiver, be set in just the right location, or even be accessing a different network. When you're troubleshooting a wireless connection, it makes sense to get as close to the router as you can, certainly in the same room if it's in your own home, so you can eliminate signal strength as a possible issue.

In order to prevent every stranger who walks by from accessing any network with WiFi capability, there are a number of security options that can be set on WiFi routers. The most common of these is simply enabling password protection, so that any laptop trying to connect to the network will have to provide a password for the initial connection (after that the operating system remembers the password). The standard security for most routers today is WPA (WiFi Protected Access) with the long key (128 bits) requiring a longer password and offering somewhat better protection than the older WEP (Wireless Equivalent Privacy) implementations. Many routers come with a default key printed on the label of the router in Hex (numbers 1-9 and letters A-F), either 10 or 26 characters long, depending on the level of security. If the router allows you to create your own password (using the full keyboard character set), the equivalent password will be 5 characters for the lower security level or 13 characters for the 128 bit key. WEP security can be cracked by anybody who downloads the right software and has the patience to set up within range of your router and spy on the traffic. But it usually works well enough to keep the neighbors from eating all of your bandwidth by using your high-speed connection to download movies and play games.

Some high speed Internet providers ship wireless routers with the security enabled and don't bother to tell the customers about the encryption key on the bottom until they call technical support complaining they can't connect to their own network. More frequently, a family will pay somebody to come in and set up a wireless router in their home, or the original network may have been set up by a friend or family member who isn't around anymore. That person could have entered the password for the computers present in the home or business at that time, but when a new laptop is purchased or an existing computer loses its software settings, that password will have to be entered again. First, try the key printed on the router label, but if a custom password was created when the network was set up, you'll either have to find the piece of paper where it was written or chase the person who set up the network. If the password absolutely can't be recovered, search the Internet for how to reset the router (varies with brand), create a new password and enter it on all the computers that use the connection.

In some cases, it's easy to reset the password or turn the security on and off by connecting directly to the router with an Ethernet cable and typing the fixed IP address for the router into your browser. In recent years, manufactured Ethernet cables supplied with PC equipment have been yellow, and while color doesn't serve as an absolute identification, it might help you find the cable in a box of stuff you never use. Connecting directly by cable to the router is an important troubleshooting step for wireless connectivity even if you don't have a password problem. If you can't connect to the Internet even after plugging directly into the router, neither the wireless adapter in your laptop nor the wireless transceiver in the router are at fault. If you plug directly into the router via the Ethernet cable and you gain access to the Internet, you can continue troubleshooting wireless issues. Check Device Manager to see if it's complaining about the network hardware. If not, and you still can't gain access at this point, the problem is either with the high speed modem and ISP, or a networking software issue within the operating system.

High speed modems, often called routers if they include a built-in router, are equipped with a series of status LEDs that can be used to diagnose many connectivity problems. Whether you have a cable modem connecting to the cable company, DSL via the phone company or one of the more esoteric high speed modems, they should always include an LED that tells you if the connection between the modem and the Internet has been established. If this link light is out, or has changed colors, say from the familiar green to an ominous red, power down the modem and turn it back on again. This hard reset will usually fix dropped connection problems caused by storms, power surges or signal interruptions, providing the modem hasn't been damaged. A modem/router will also include a status LED to show whether an Ethernet cable connection to your laptop is good, and your laptop will have a little status/activity LED for the network connection as well. While color coding isn't universal, solid green usually indicates a good connection, and blinking green or orange usually indicates activity. Some modems include an LED to tell you if the DSL or cable link to the ISP is good even when the Internet isn't functioning.

Operating system issues affecting connectivity can include firewall (security software) settings that prevent your computer from establishing communications with the Internet Service Provider (ISP), or the failure to install the software that ISP requires. Unfortunately, there are also more complicated problems that will require drawn out conversations with the ISP's technical support department to troubleshoot. If you're adventurous, or desperate, you'll find all sorts of third party software online that will reset the Windows stack or change registry settings back to defaults, but you're better off trying the tech support route first if a software glitch is at the bottom of your problems. Also, some older versions of Windows that supported WiFi did so through some software applications provided by the wireless adapter manufacturer rather than through the operating system. Setting up wireless communications on these older systems can require steps unfamiliar to the typical user who expects Windows to go out and find the new wireless connection without operator help.

Troubleshooting Motherboard, CPU and Memory

The most expensive and hardest to replace component in your laptop is the motherboard. The expense isn't due to the intrinsic complexity. Motherboards for desktop computers are more capable and cost much less. Laptop motherboards are expensive because they are unique to the model and the brand, and no generic replacements are available. If the motherboard fails, your choice is to buy a new one from the manufacturer at a price that will cost about as much as buying a new consumer grade laptop, or to look for one in the used market. Oftentimes, people sell their old laptops on eBay "for parts only", just like you might sell a car that can't pass inspection, and as long as you don't pay much you aren't taking a big risk.

Motherboard failures are among the hardest to diagnose with a high degree of confidence because all of the components in the laptop are connected to the motherboard one way or another. When confronted with a dead laptop, you'll find that our diagnostics send you through all of the major subsystems before considering the motherboard. Sometimes, the only way for a home user to positively identify that a problem is with the motherboard and not with a component is to test that component in another computer, or swap in a known good component to test the laptop. For example, any number of failures related to the hard drive can turn out to be due to the failure of the hard drive controller or the connector, both of which are part of the motherboard. The same goes for the DVD, the keyboard, the RAM or the CPU. In some cases, as with a display problem, you can use an external monitor to test if the video processor on the motherboard is functioning properly. But with a drive failure, you may not know for sure if it's the drive or the motherboard until you test the drive separately.

Fortunately, total motherboard failures aren't regular occurrences, barring physical abuse of the laptop such as dropping it or spilling drinks. You're more likely to encounter a connector problem with the motherboard, like the power jack breaking a solder joint, then a true electronic blow-out. One of the most problematic motherboard components, the RAM, is normally socketed and easily accessible through a hatch on the bottom of the laptop. Since the motherboard can't function without the RAM, most technicians will try replacing it before they even start the troubleshooting process. The motherboard is equally helpless if the CPU has failed, but in many instances the CPU is permanently soldered to the motherboard, and it can be a laborious replacement task even if it's socketed. While you probably don't have a spare CPU of the proper type lying about, RAM is very cheap and replacing it is perhaps the easiest job you can do on a laptop. If two memory modules are installed in your laptop, you can test them by taking out the second one, and then swapping the two if the motherboard still appears to be dead.

Intermittent failure of the motherboard, CPU or memory is nearly impossible to properly diagnose without swapping parts, but if overheating is involved, you can make some educated guesses. If the video goes wonky when the laptop is hot, the problem is likely the RAM or the video processor (which is usually a motherboard component). We briefly discuss some of the garage technician hacks for certain video processor failures in the notes for video troubleshooting. If you get total lock-ups or blue screens of death when the laptop heats up, the problem is often the RAM or the CPU.

In many models laptop manufacturers employ daughter cards, which are independent circuit cards that attach to the motherboard and provide functions like wireless, a dial-up modem, and Ethernet. Some designs also put the graphics processor on a daughter card. The use of a communications daughter card, especially modems which are often damaged by lightning strikes, allows for a cost effective replacement if the laptop isn't too old. Until you research your model on the web you won't know for sure what functions are integrated on your motherboard or which daughter cards might be included. A second hand video daughter card can go as cheap as $20 on eBay, so it's always worth checking if your video is integrated on the motherboard or on a separate daughter card before making any decisions.

Replacing the motherboard in a laptop is no cakewalk for a trained technician who has never worked on the particular model, and it's a multi-hour task for a gifted beginner with good illustrated instructions. Assuming the replacement motherboard is good, there are still a large number of things that can go wrong, from forcing screws into the wrong holes to breaking delicate cable connectors that aren't designed for repetitive use or rough handling. Due to the cramped geometry and the relative fragility of the cables, it's very easy to accidentally break a conductor while doing the work, introducing a new problem that will be difficult to troubleshoot.

In some instances, your laptop will diagnose its own problem and produce a text message or beep code (a series of beeps when you power on the laptop). Looking up those beep codes on the manufacturer's website should tell you if there's a definitive problem with the motherboard that will require its replacement, or indicate a problem with the CPU or memory. Memory problems are easily resolved by replacing the RAM module, but CPU problems are often caused by the failure of a direct CPU cooling system. Engineers don't have very much flexibility in building cooling systems for laptop CPUs due to the cramped space and low headroom. The CPU will always be equipped with a finned metal heatsink, and either there will be a fan mounted on the heatsink to draw off the heat, or the heatsink will be located in the air flow generated by a remote fan and directed through a fan hood. Before replacing a CPU, it's worthwhile to try reseating it in its socket and reinstalling the heatsink with a fresh layer of thermal paste. Also, you should confirm that the fan cooling the heatsink is operating, either visually or through feeling the airflow.

Troubleshooting Laptop Dial-Up Modems

Even if you've been using high speed Internet access at home for years, you might still find yourself in need of dial-up when traveling outside large cities or taking a summer vacation. If your Internet connection is the basic infrastructure of your business life, you can't wander out in the rain looking for a café with free wireless every time you need access. Dial-up access at 56Kbs is surprisingly good for both e-mail and general web work, as long as you don't have to deal with large attachments, video, or audio files. Some day, when wireless access is truly omnipresent, laptop manufacturers may do away with dial-up modems, but until then, they are an indispensable feature for many laptop buyers.

Some laptop manufacturers now offer built-in cellular modems, but there remain several drawbacks to these. First, the cellular providers in the US use different technologies, so the built-in modem will probably only work with a single provider. This in turn forces you to sign a contract with that provider to use the built-in modem even if you use a different cellular provider for your phone, who would have offered a voice/data package deal. Cellular Internet access remains expensive, with prices ranging from around $50 to $80 a month, depending on the carrier, length of contract, and package deal. Signing a two year contract for cellular Internet access is likely a greater investment than purchasing the laptop. Also, regular WiFi (which is free in many locations) is much faster than cellular

Internet access, and cellular access comes with restrictions for heavy users. Finally, it's easy enough to buy a cellular modem and plug it into your laptops PC card slot, which you aren't likely to be using for anything else, and a cellular modem may even come free when you sign a contract with your carrier.

If you go back far enough in time, say the mid-1990's, there were laptops being sold without an internal dial-up modem. Getting online required an old serial port external modem or a special adapter, often a PCMCIA card. These days, all laptops have a built-in 56Kbs dial-up modem, and serial ports and parallel ports have been replaced by USB ports. Inexpensive modems that include fax capabilities are still available in USB versions as replacement modems for laptops. When it comes to hardware failure, external modems are easier to troubleshoot than internal modems because you can always try an external modem on another laptop or PC to see if it still works.

Dial-up problems usually have nothing to do with the modem hardware itself. The more common causes are service provider issues, ranging from hardware failures with their modem pool or their Internet backbone connection, to your having forgot to pay the bill and getting locked out of your account. If you can hear the modem dial the phone, and the result is something other than a whistle, your problem isn't with your modem hardware. If you hear the dialing but the dial tone never alters, you're probably dialing with tone on an old pulse only system. If the phone rings on the other end, and a voice picks up or you get a recorded message, you're dialing the wrong number. If the modems connect to each other (lots of whistling and hissing) but you fail to get on, it's most likely an invalid username or password. In all instances, when you are troubleshooting modem problems, you should enable the modem audio, so you can hear what's going on.

Most modems are set up to dial only when they hear a dial tone, so if you aren't plugged into a live phone jack, you're unlikely to hear anything. The first test for troubleshooting dial-up problems is to try dialing with a regular telephone on the wall jack you are using, and then take the telephone cord out of that phone and plug it right into your laptop modem port for testing. This eliminates the chance that your modem patch cord is faulty, or that the output port on the phone, FAX or other phone connected device you were plugged into isn't really passing through the live line. Never assume that a phone jack is good just because it exists. Houses all over the world are full of extension jacks for phones that have never worked, were never tested, or were cut off decades ago. If there's an easily accessible network interface box for testing a phone outside the house, it's a good way to troubleshoot whether a line problem is in the house or the responsibility of the phone company.

If your problem isn't with getting connected but with staying connected, the problem likely lies outside of your laptop. In some cases, the modem you are connected to in the service provider modem pool will be bad, or connected to a flaky power source, or employing a "dump for inactivity" scheme. More frequently, you may find that your connection is slow or fragile at certain times of day, or during weather events. In the former case, telephone trunk lines get noisier (electrically) during peak activity periods, which may include first thing in the morning, after school and after supper hours. Weather events, from rain to wind, can degrade line conditions over a period of time or lead to frequent disconnects. The best indication that you are dealing with an environmental or service provider problem rather than a laptop hardware issue is if the problem only occurs from time to time.

However, there are some failures that will be attributed to either the modem hardware in the laptop or the driver software that supports it. All Windows based systems come equipped with decent troubleshooting for modems in Control Panel, though the exact sequence and tab labels to arrive at the diagnostics vary from Windows 95 up through Vista. A modem that passes the Windows diagnostic is almost never bad, though the connection can certainly suffer if the laptop experiences overheating problems. If the modem fails the Windows diagnostic, or if the modem is identified as a problem in Windows Device Manager, the first step is to find the current driver for the modem on the manufacturer's website and reinstall it. If Windows can't find the modem, it's a hardware failure. Some manufacturers, in their modem troubleshooting suggestions, may suggest that you upgrade the laptop BIOS by flashing the latest version. This shouldn't be necessary unless you've upgraded the operating system and there's a known problem with the old BIOS documented on the Internet. Remember that a simple work-around in the form of a USB modem is always available, and doesn't risk turning your laptop into a useless brick.

If your laptop frequently locks up or freezes online, there are two basic possibilities. If hitting CRTL-ALT-DEL allows you to bring up the task list and close the connection, the problem is due to the way your browser, e-mail, or other internet application reacts to time-outs or other dial-up issues. But if you're getting a blue screen of death or the laptop doesn't respond to CTRL-ALT-DEL, it's likely an issue with overheating or the motherboard, CPU or RAM. Laptops generally implement their modems in software, rather than including a DSP (Digital Signal Processing) chip, which means that the CPU and motherboard are doing double duty when the modem is in use, and it could be just enough to push a marginal heat problem into the red. Don't think in terms of motherboard replacement if there's a possible overheating, motherboard or CPU problem (RAM is easily replaceable) that only manifests itself during dial-up modem use or if the modem port breaks off the motherboard. You aren't giving up any convenience or mobility by using a USB modem, as they are quite small and you're tied to a phone line in any case.

A final tip is that many laptop makers put the dial-up modem, wireless, and Ethernet networking together on a daughter card. If all of these fail at the same time, a problem with the daughter card is a good bet.

Troubleshooting DVD/CD Playback and Record

Laptops have standardized on a DVD/CD recorder and player being a standard feature, with the exception of the lightest and most expensive models. If your laptop is a couple years old, you may have a DVD player combined with a CD recorder, or even just a DVD and CD player. You'd have to go back to around 2001 for laptops manufactured with just a CD player, and most of those still had a built-in floppy drive. Some higher end laptops intended for travel use put the DVD player in a swappable bay, so it can be easily changed for a second battery which extends the laptop's unplugged life to a full business day, but a few models only support external DVD drives. Another swappable bay option is a second hard drive, handy for secure work environments where the data doesn't leave the office, or for power users doing video editing on the road. There may even be a floppy drive option available, if you can see the point of swapping out your DVD recorder for a floppy drive. Laptops with swappable bays usually feature "Hot Swapping" which allows you to swap bay components without powering off the laptop. It's neat technology, but read the owner's manual carefully before giving it a go.

If you own an older laptop, the simplest troubleshooting step for laptop burners (DVD or CD recorders) is determining whether or not one is present. DVD/CD drives are usually labeled with multiple icons right on the outside face of the tray that detail the capabilities of the drive. If the icons show "Reader" or "ROM" rather than "RW" or "Recorder", you may be looking at an older laptop without recording functionality. Another giveaway is the installed software. Laptops with disc burners will ship with recording software, often times with both the laptop manufacturer's recording software and a third party recording package. At least one laptop model comes fresh from the factory with three different ways to record DVDs. The software packages may have different strengths and weaknesses. For example, the manufacturer software is usually there for recording basic data discs and for creating a back-up image of the laptop hard drive, if the laptop didn't ship with recovery media. Another software package might be designed for creating and replicating both CDs and DVDs for general use, while a third application might handle creating photo DVD's for your television player, or home movies. If you purchase a third party recording package, you may find that you have to update the DVD recorder firmware before it will work with the drive. This firmware upgrade is similar to the BIOS Flash upgrade in terms of the underlying process, but it's safer because the firmware only affects the DVD or CD recorder, and can be retried if it fails.

Optical drive
emergency release:

www.fonerbooks.com
/laptop12.htm

One of the worst failures you can encounter with your drive is when the tray simply won't eject. While the operating system is running, the drive may be locked or disabled in software, but when you first power on the system, the tray should pop out pretty quickly in response to hitting the eject button. There are a few reasons a tray will fail to eject. If the drive isn't properly seated in the bay it may be mechanically binding or not connected to power. If the drive is in a swappable bay, try removing it and reinstalling, and make sure that the release latch snaps to the locked position when it's installed. If the drive is permanently mounted, it shouldn't break free of its connector unless it's not secured in place. This can happen if the laptop is secured with a single screw which was removed in an earlier repair and never replaced. Loose drive failures can creep on you. The drive can function and stay in place for months without being secured, because it's a tight fit and the power/data connector tends to hold it in place.

If the tray doesn't eject even when the drive is seated properly, the last resort is to power down and use the emergency release pinhole on the front faceplate. You can do this with the drive installed in the bay, but if it's the swappable type, it's easier to do with the drive out and on the table. Straighten out a length of a paperclip that's just thin enough to fit through the hole, and gently insert it. Listen for the release click and try to feel it through your fingers. When the tray releases, it may spring out half inch, or it may barely move at all, so you have to get a hold of the front of the tray to pull it out. If a disc has come apart in the drive, either because it shattered or a stick-on label lifted off, getting all the bits out and getting it working again isn't a high probability, so don't test it with a disc of any value after attempting the repair. If it's an electrical/mechanical failure of the ejector mechanism, repairing it yourself isn't practical.

Unless you typically use your laptop to watch movies or listen to music CDs while traveling, you may find it is less painful to get by without one than to buy a factory replacement for an older model. Thanks to the availability of inexpensive external DVD/CD recorders for USB, you can bypass the internal drive and just plug in the USB drive when you need to record a disc or install a new program. The nice thing about an external USB drive is you'll be able to use it on different laptops and desktop PCs as long as it lasts, while an internal laptop drive generally requires an exact replacement for that model family.

Another note for movie fans. All new laptop DVDs should play legal copies of DVD movies without any special actions being required on your part. When a DVD drive works with some discs but won't play movies, the fault is almost always in the decoding software, known as a CODEC (Coder/DECoder). Anything that changes the support software for your media player, including automated operating system updates, might render your current CODEC useless. In this case you to must go on the web and download a new version before movies will play again. Because most playback and recording problems are software specific and impact a large number of users, you can save a lot of time by researching the problem on the Internet.

The most common read failure for DVD/CD players is dirty or damaged discs. Because the discs hold up so well, some people have gotten into the habit of not storing them in their envelopes or jewel boxes. You've probably seen discs stacked in mounds in drawers or strewn in messy piles on desks, yet they seem to work most of the time when needed. But when your laptop won't read a particular CD or DVD, the first thing to do is to clean it with a nice lint free cloth, flannel shirts work well, and inspect it for scratches and surface build-up, like jelly donut stains. If cleaning the disc works, you've found your problem, but if it doesn't, check whether or not the drive will read a nice factory fresh movie or music disc. You can try using a drive cleaning kit of the type sold in office stores or online, but don't spend a lot because they usually don't fix the problem.

In rare cases, a DVD/CD hardware failure might announce itself during boot with a text line reporting something like "DVD drive failure" or the drive may disappear from CMOS Setup. If the hardware isn't aware that the drive is installed, the operating system software isn't going to have much of a chance. These types of hardware errors either mean the drive electronics have failed and aren't communicating, the drive has become dislodged from the connector in the drive bay, or the controller/cable on the motherboard has failed. The only other problem likely to announce itself is a loud, vibrating drive. If you notice your drive making more noise than usual or making the whole laptop tremble, stop what you're doing and hit the eject button. The usual cause is an off balance disk, either because it was seated wrong in the tray, was manufactured poorly (especially stick on labels), or has some foreign matter stuck to it. It's not worth destroying your drive trying to read a shaky disc. If you must try, do it in a PC drive that's built heavier and is easier to replace if the disc comes apart. Note also that some laptops offer a "quiet drive" feature so it won't be a distraction while playing entertainment discs, which should be turned off while troubleshooting.

Recording problems are occasionally related to hardware failures, but more often than not, they are due to the user stubbornly trying to record on some faulty media. Software problems or protection schemes involved in duplicating manufactured discs are also a leading cause of failed recordings. Never give up on a recorder based on one stack of "100% guaranteed" blank discs purchased on a spool. Try a fresh disc from a friend, and ask the friend to test one of your discs. If your drive refuses to acknowledge that you've inserted a disc suitable for recording, the disc may be the wrong type, it may be recorded and closed already, or it may be faulty. If it's the cheaper unlabeled media, you may even be installing it in the drive upside-down.

If your recording sessions take forever to start, make sure that your virus software isn't scanning every file before it can be prepared for writing to the disc. If your recording sessions always end in failure, it could be the media, but more likely it's caused by the drive buffer running out of data because the laptop CPU is busy with other tasks. Try recording first thing after you turn on the laptop, with your Internet connection disconnected (turn off wireless or unplug your laptop from the modem/router). Before attempting the third or fourth time, use task manager to check the CPU utilization, and stop other tasks that are running and eating up resources.

A particularly frustrating problem is when your DVD/CD drive refuses to boot an operating system disc or recovery disc after a system failure. Check that the disc is bootable in another computer. If the disc is good, try changing the boot order in CMOS Setup so that the DVD/CD drive is checked before the BIOS hands over control to the hard drive. This is particularly effective if a virus or data corruption has rendered the hard drive partially bootable, so the laptop keeps trying the hard drive but never fully succeeds. If the DVD/CD drive is good, it will boot bootable discs, so assuming the disc is clean and bootable, proceed with troubleshooting as if it were a normal read failure.

Troubleshooting Laptop Sound

If you can't get any sound out of your laptop, the most likely cause is the volume being turned down or muted. Newer laptops monitor the exterior sound control so when the volume is turned up or down manually, the volume control in the operating system tracks right along with it. But with some laptops, especially those with exterior dial volume controls rather than toggles, the volume dials are independent of the software volume control and can't be monitored in software. In this case, if the volume dial is turned down on the outside of the laptop, the sound is turned off and no amount of monkeying around in the operating system can change that.

Unfortunately, checking the external volume control on the laptop and the standard laptop volume slider in the operating system (the icon is a little speaker in Windows system tray) doesn't eliminate all volume problems. Depending on the software installed and what you are trying to do, there may still be multiple volume controls and mixer panels scattered about the operating system. If the wrong channel is muted or turned down all the way in one of these independent controls, the laptop isn't going to produce sound. The first sign most laptop users get that their audio isn't working is the absence of operating system sounds, like the Windows rush on start up, or chimes with e-mail activity. Of course, these sounds can be turned off by design as well, through the Sounds option in Windows Control Panel. So, before looking at hardware problems, another hunting expedition is necessary to make sure the software is supposed to be playing sounds.

If you try to play an audio CD and the media player shows that the song is progressing but you can't get any sound out of the laptop speakers, odds are that the volume is turned down or muted. But occasionally, the onboard sound hardware will fail. If you are confident the volume is turned on in all possible locations and you've checked Windows Device Manager for a report of a hardware failure, try listening through headphones. Laptops are all equipped with external audio jacks for a microphone and headphones, and some might include an additional jack for "line" to pass the playback to a home entertainment system. If the headphones work, the wiring to the internal speakers has broken or come loose. Wiring failure is only likely if the speakers are in the lid and therefore wired through the hinges.

If you don't get any sound out of the headphones and you haven't missed a "mute" being checked off somewhere in software controls, it really is a hardware failure. If the problem is with all sounds, including Windows chimes, internet radio, etc, then the problem is that the integrated sound processor has failed. Unless the sound system is on a daughter card, it means the fix would require replacing the motherboard. But if the only thing you can't do is play audio CD's, the problem is that the output from the DVD/CD player is muted or not getting to the amplification stage.

In modern laptops the DVD/CD players feature Digital Audio Extraction (DAE) which means that music CDs can be read digitally and the data passed to the built-in sound card or an external sound card replacement. In older laptops, music CDs weren't digitally "read" by the system, they were played by the CD player, which produced an analog sound output that was passed to the laptop's sound system for amplification. With both the old and the new players, if there's a problem with the DVD/CD connector or if the wiring has been damaged, the music CD may get spun around without the sound making it to amplification. With the old fashioned players, if the little D/A (Digital/Analog) converter chip in the DVD/CD player is blown, the only way you'll be able to play music CDs is to replace the drive. The modern DAE output rarely fails on the drive, but the connector can fail. Make sure that digital playback is enabled in the properties tab of the drive.

USB speaker work-around:

www.fonerbooks.com
/speakers.htm

You can replace your built-in laptop sound card with a PC card, with a USB sound card or USB speakers. The main audience for laptop sound card replacements is people who want to turn their laptop into a home entertainment center, with 5.1 or 7.1 surround sound. For our purposes, these replacements make good workarounds if the integrated audio system fails.

They also bring with them a whole new level of software with more volume controls, which hopefully is well integrated with the existing operating system software. When shopping for replacement sound cards, keep in mind that USB solutions are much cheaper than PC cards. You need a laptop PC card, not a sound card for a PC, which will usually be PCI technology. The laptop peripheral manufacturers who agreed on the name "PC card" for a laptop add-on did a disservice to consumers the world over who have doubtlessly made uncounted purchasing errors. Also, when purchasing USB speakers to replace the laptop's sound system, don't buy speakers advertised as "USB powered". The "USB powered" speakers only draw their power from the USB port, they still need to be plugged into a regular audio jack to play anything.

Microphones and headsets have become an important part of laptop sound systems with the rise of Internet telephony, video conferencing and voice recognition. The quality of the microphone input depends both on the microphone itself and the integrated laptop sound card. If you're using a good microphone and you just can't get the quality or volume you need for your application, the laptop sound card hardware is probably at fault. It's not a failure per se, as long as it functions well enough to play music CDs and operating system sounds. It's just not good enough for your application. The two options are to purchase a quality USB microphone system, which effectively bypasses the laptops built-in sound system, or to go with a USB or PC card replacement sound card and plug in a regular microphone.

Wired Network Troubleshooting

Given the WiFi capability built-into modern laptops it may seem unnecessary to discuss wired LANs (Local Area Networks) in a laptop book. In fact, most of the troubleshooting steps in the accompanying flowchart are primarily intended for medium sized business or wired school networks. Many employees today are commuting with machines owned by their employer, which plug into wired networks when at the office, and not a few people are adding the laptop to an existing home office LAN that also supports desktop PCs and printers. Yes, one solution is to add a wireless router to the LAN, and then connect the laptop via wireless. But this means buying and configuring a new piece of equipment, and from a security standpoint, a wired LAN is safer because physical access to the building is required to intercept traffic. Also, wired network connections remain much faster than standard WiFi connections, provided all of your network hardware is up to date.

The main culprit with wired networking is the wiring, or more specifically, the RJ-45 connectors that look like overgrown phone connectors on the wire ends. RJ-45 connectors are in reality overgrown phone connectors, and they have taken over the networking field to the extent that we don't even talk about older coaxial networking or corporate fiber optic cabling in this section. The RJ-45 connectors are universally crimp-ons. As there's no soldering or clamping involved, the connection is only as good as the crimp. There's a crush-in stress relief on the connector to help keep the conductors from moving around on the crimp contacts when the cable gets tugged on.

One of the winning points of twisted pair networking was its flexibility and ease of installation. Pull a standard wire, crimp on a connector, and you're done. But the very flexibility of the system leads to people pulling on the cords, flopping them over desks, forgetting they are attached and trying to move the laptop. This can cause the port to break off the board inside the laptop, or it may weaken the connector. Cheap crimping tools have encouraged many people to make their own cables, without ever learning how they are supposed to be made. At the core of twisted pair networking, whether 10BaseT, 100BaseT or 1000BaseT (Gigabit), are twisted pairs of wire which provide electrical insulation from noise by carrying differential signals (the noise cancels out). If you don't make the cables properly, the network may limp over very short distances at low speeds, but will fail on longer runs or higher speed.

In addition, there are statutory length limits for different types of twisted pair networks. You can't reel out a half-mile of cable, put connectors on the ends and expect it to work. The maximum length specified is one hundred meters, or a little over 300 ft. You might squeeze out a little more distance with a high quality cable in an electrically quiet environment, but the signaling strength isn't engineered for long distances. The slower the network, the more tolerant it will be of poorly made cables, pair splitting and failing connectors. Some networking adapters and hubs will automatically lower the connection speed under poor conditions, but it's not a situation to aspire to. Better to just fix it and run at the hardware's maximum speed.

Network adapters, routers and hubs are equipped with LEDs that show the link status and activity. Don't assume that because a hub or a router is working with other computers and the link LED for your cable is lit, everything must be OK. Individual ports on hubs and routers can fail with the link LED remaining lit, so try another port, even if it means temporarily disconnecting another computer. Positive link status just means there's a cable attached between the hub port and the laptop and it's not broken. But that LED is a useful tool. If you see the green link LED flicker when you wiggle the wire at either end, it's a sign that either the RJ-45 connector is loose, or the port in the laptop or the hub or router is bad.

Moving past hardware issues, software is the crazy aunt in the wire closet of networking. In the absence of expert help, your best bet is to find a similar machine on the network, ideally running the same version of the operating system, and clone the settings it's using. The exception is if the network is set up with fixed network addresses, in which you'll need to get your full designated address from the network administrator, which is a good time to ask for help. The problem could be as simple as a mistyped workgroup name on a peer-to-peer network, or misspelling the username or password received from the network administrator on a business network.

The most common wired networking connection in the home is between the laptop and the high speed modem/router. Some Internet service providers don't supply free wireless routers, and some users prefer the security of a hard wired connection and turn off the router's wireless capability. If you can't access the Internet through your direct network connection to the router, it's very possible that the router itself has lost contact with the Internet and needs to be reset.

Troubleshooting Keyboard, Pointer and USB

Perhaps the most important thing you can learn about your keyboard, touchpad, and even your USB ports, is that they can all be bypassed. Most laptops offer either a PS/2 or proprietary

Laptop key replacement:

www.fonerbooks.com /laptop15.htm

port for an external keyboard and mouse (it may have to be manually enabled in CMOS Setup), and you can always buy inexpensive USB keyboards, mice, and other pointers to use. If all of your USB ports should fail (a very rare occurrence) you can buy a replacement USB adapter as a laptop PC card. If the problem is with the USB ports being mechanically broken inside the laptop by repeated abuse, you can still use the integrated USB through a port replicator or docking station. So the bottom line is, you don't have to rush to replace your laptop keyboard or pointing device should the hardware fail or simply wear out.

You may notice a problem with your keyboard when some repeated characteristic spelling error appears, like you keep on leaving the letter "a" out of words. After a while, you figure out that you're spelling them right, it's just that hitting the "a" key doesn't always result in an "a" showing up on the screen. The spills and crumbs that get into the keyboard and remain there often gang up with lint and hair to gum up the workings of certain keys. As long as the problem is with foreign matter gumming up the retaining clip that holds the key in place and not with the actual key contact, which is sealed within the keyboard membrane, you can fix it. That is, provided you can figure out how to remove the key with destroying the retaining clip, and you have good enough manual dexterity to put it back together again after you remove the built up crud.

The difficulty of replacing the entire keyboard membrane (the keys come attached) varies from laptop to laptop, depending on whether you can easily access it from the top side, without messing with the hinges. If the keyboard disappears entirely from Device Manager it could indicate that that the motherboard controller has failed, in which case, investing in a replacement membrane is a pretty big risk. A warning in Device Manager may also indicate that the ribbon connector has come undone or failed, though that's pretty rare unless you've had the laptop apart. The replacement membrane with keys usually costs less than $100, but if you normally use the laptop in one location and you don't have any repair experience, it's less risky to just start using a USB keyboard. Probably the handiest laptop accessory around is the USB splitter, which allows you to plug a standard mouse and keyboard into the laptop, rather than buying expensive versions with proprietary connectors from the manufacturer.

More laptops come equipped with a touchpad than any other pointing device. Touchpads can take a while for new users to get used to, and they tend to come overloaded with shortcut commands. If you're getting frustrated with your touchpad because it keeps launching applications when you're just trying to move the pointer on the screen, you need to adjust the software settings. There may be a touchpad icon with all the options in the system tray, and you can always find it in Windows Control Panel. Many users are most comfortable with all of the extra functionality disabled, including tapping on the touchpad to click the mouse. If the physical buttons for clicking don't work as you expected, their functionality can also be changed in the touchpad settings. If neither the buttons nor the touchpad work at all, make sure they are enabled in software. If Device Manager can't see the touchpad, there's a good chance the controller has failed or the cable has worked off.

USB is one of the great successes of modern computer standards, allowing manufacturers to design tens of thousands of different products that can be attached to your laptop by one standard cable to a standard port. If it wasn't for the software, USB would be practically idiot proof. Unfortunately, the USB interface only provides the path for the laptop and the attached device to talk to each other, the software still has to be right for the conversation to make any sense. The first step in troubleshooting USB problems is to simplify the setup. Plug the device directly into a USB port on your laptop, without daisy chaining through other USB devices, hubs, docking stations or port replicators. Once you get it working, you can try a more torturous cabling route and find out if there's a problem somewhere in the middle.

USB splitter for laptop:

www.fonerbooks.com /r_usb.htm

The majority of USB ports on laptops in use today are either USB 2.0 or USB 1.1, a successful earlier version. USB 2.0 is much faster than USB 1.1 and handles power differently, so some devices sold for USB 2.0 will not be backwards compatible, and will work very poorly if at all. All USB 1.1 devices should work on USB 2.0 ports, and the new USB 3.0 ports should be able to handle all of the older devices as well. The higher the communication speed of the device, the more important you use a quality cable. The USB port and cable wiring is actually quite simple, a ground, a +5.0 V power supply, and two signal conductors carrying a differential (plus and minus) signal for noise isolation.

The main hazard to USB ports is that the cables end up end up all over the place and get yanked on. People can trip over them and you may jerk the laptop around moving your feet under the table. The worst punishment for the USB port is if you forget that you have a USB cable plugged into the laptop, close the lid, and trying to walk away with it. This abuse can lead to broken solder joints inside the laptop, and bent ports that only create the proper connection if you hold the cable just so. If the USB port feels loose inside the laptop, it's broken. The whole laptop is put in danger if somebody trips over the cable and pulls it off the table. The cables themselves are fairly bullet proof, normally inflicting more damage than they absorb, but a high heeled shoe or desk drawer can damage a cable and break the conductors. So you shouldn't assume a cable is good unless you've tested it with another device on your laptop, and remember that cheaper cables may work with older USB standards but not the new faster ones. Never try using a USB cable if the plastic spacer in the connector is missing. It can short out the port and damage the motherboard.

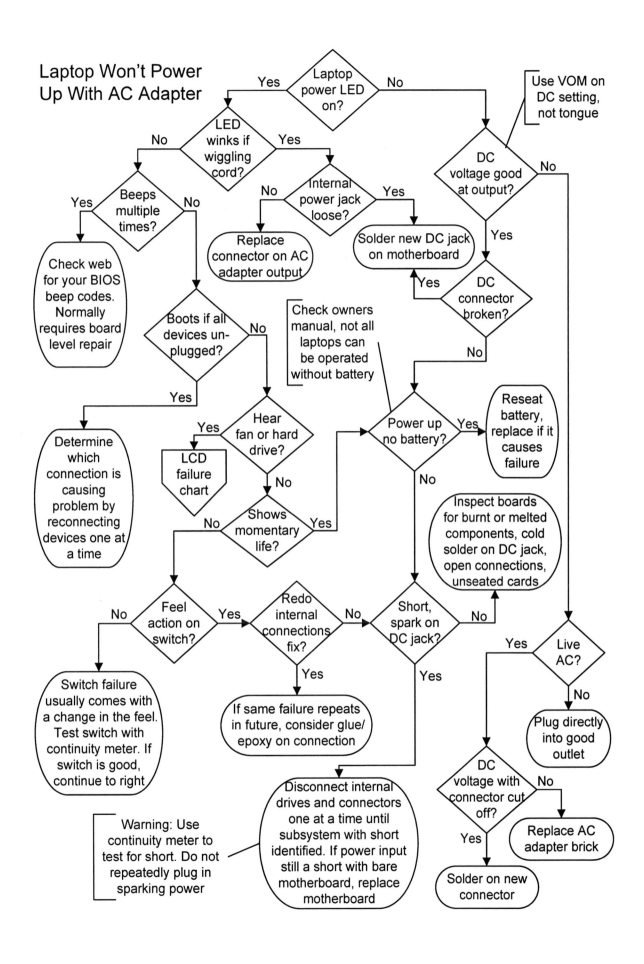

Laptop Won't Power
Up With AC Adapter

Laptop power LED on?

Use VOM on DC setting, not tongue

LED winks if wiggling cord?

Beeps multiple times?

Check web for your BIOS beep codes. Normally requires board level repair

Internal power jack loose?

Replace connector on AC adapter output

Solder new DC jack on motherboard

DC voltage good at output?

DC connector broken?

Boots if all devices un-plugged?

Check owners manual, not all laptops can be operated without battery

Determine which connection is causing problem by reconnecting devices one at a time

Hear fan or hard drive?

LCD failure chart

Power up no battery?

Reseat battery, replace if it causes failure

Shows momentary life?

Inspect boards for burnt or melted components, cold solder on DC jack, open connections, unseated cards

Feel action on switch?

Redo internal connections fix?

Short, spark on DC jack?

Live AC?

Switch failure usually comes with a change in the feel. Test switch with continuity meter. If switch is good, continue to right

If same failure repeats in future, consider glue/ epoxy on connection

Plug directly into good outlet

Warning: Use continuity meter to test for short. Do not repeatedly plug in sparking power

Disconnect internal drives and connectors one at a time until subsystem with short identified. If power input still a short with bare motherboard, replace motherboard

DC voltage with connector cut off?

Replace AC adapter brick

Solder on new connector

Laptop power LED on? Laptops come equipped with a series of LEDs, often above the keyboard or on the front edge, that display the status or activity of laptop sub-systems. There are normally separate LEDs that will light when the AC adapter is plugged in, when the battery is charging, and when the laptop is powered on. In addition, there may be LEDs for hard drive and wireless activity and for DVD or CD action. Some laptops even feature a power button that lights when the power is turned on. In this particular diagnostic step, we're interested in the LED that shows that external power is connected, which is occasionally the same as the LED that shows the battery is charging. These are the only LEDs that should be lit when the laptop isn't turned on but is plugged into a live AC adapter.

LED winks if wiggling cord? If the LED showing that power is connected or that the battery is charging winks and blinks when you wiggle the cord plugged into the laptop, you have a bad electrical connection. The result is often that the power supplied is too intermittent to charge the battery or carry the system though a power on cycle, unless the cord is in the perfect position. If the LED blinks or flickers when you aren't wiggling the cord, check the owner's manual for what it's trying to tell you. It could indicate a bad or unrecognized battery, or a problem with the AC adapter output. While you will test for these as you go along, checking the manufacturer user manual first can save you time.

Internal power jack loose? In cases of total failure, it's usually a broken center pin or a failed solder joint on the board. This can even happen with relatively new laptops if the solder joint was poor quality to start with and the high electrical resistance led to further overheating of the joint until it failed. But the most common reason for mechanical failure of the power jack inside the laptop is unintentional abuse. Problems include: pulling out the connector at an angle when disconnecting the power, careless movement of other items on the desk pulling the cord around while it's plugged in, dropping the laptop with adapter attached or stepping on the cord.

Simply letting the cord droop all of the time if you work on your lap is much more likely to lead to the failure of the external connector than the internal port. The easiest way to test if the connector on the end of the AC adapter cord is failing is to measure the DC output while having somebody wiggle the cord.

If you have alligator clips for your test leads, you can do this yourself. Failures are almost always gradual, where the laptop will operate and charge fine as long as you position the cord properly to keep the LED lit, but this gets more and more difficult with time as additional strands of wire break.

Beeps multiple times? Laptops, like desktop PCs, go through a POST (Power On Self Test) process when turned on. If the POST carried out by the BIOS detects a failure, it may report the failure through a series of beeps, whether or not it can light up the screen. These beep codes are specific to the BIOS manufacturer and are sometimes proprietary to the laptop manufacturer or model as well, but you can usually find out what they signify by Googling "Beep Code" and the brand and model of your laptop.

The downside to beep codes is they often identify problems that you can't fix. The most common beep code that you can do something about is RAM failure. If you get a beep code you can't identify and nothing seems to work, the first step is to reseat the memory module(s). If you have more than one memory module, try operating with just one, and then just the other in the first slot. You might want to gamble on buying a new memory module, using an online configurator to pick the correct module for your model, as they are pretty inexpensive. Other beep code failures are generally related to surface mount processors that can't be repaired at home, though some people have had luck with reflowing solder on video processors, using various novel techniques. If you determine you have a video processor failure on the main board and you're feeling adventurous, do a Google search on "reflow solder" and your model.

Boots if all devices unplugged? One of the easiest power problems to troubleshoot is when an external device, such as a printer, a network connection, a PCMCIA (Personal Computer Memory Card International Association) or PC card, video monitor, or even a JumpDrive or USB mouse is preventing the laptop from powering on. This may occur due to a short circuit or electrical problem in the external device or due to a problem with the mechanical movement of the port inside the notebook. It can be easily diagnosed by removing all external devices (except the AC power adapter).

Hear fan or hard drive? When one or more status LEDs on the laptop are lit, it may be that the basic power circuitry is functioning, but the boot process is being aborted before it even starts. If you can hear the hard drive spinning up or the CPU fan come on and stay on, or if the hard drive activity LED blinks away merrily, there's a good chance that the problem is isolated to the video display subsystem. One quick check is to attach an external monitor, though you may have to use a key combination, normally the master Fn (Function) key along with one of the other keys along the top of the keyboard, to tell the laptop that you want to enable the external video port.

Shows momentary signs of life? Does the hard drive spin up and stop, or can you hear the fan click on and off? Do the LED's change state when you press the power button, even for a moment? Does the screen show any changes, even just a passing ghost of an image or some bright spots along an edge? All of these may be signs of trying to power up with a battery that's stone dead or has suffered an internal failure, with a laptop that shuts itself down on "abnormal" battery conditions.

It could also be the sign of a nearly discharged battery combined with a faulty AC adapter or charging circuit. Some people have reported problems with generic after-market AC adapters that are only capable of charging the battery when the laptop is turned off. Due to low voltage or insufficient current, they simply won't operate the laptop on their own unless a charged battery is supplementing the power.

Feel action on switch? Notebook switches vary as much as keyboards in feel, but you should feel some initial resistance when you press the power switch, and there should also be a tactile switching feel. If that feel is absent or if the switch moves up and down loosely, it's probable that the switch has physically failed. Unfortunately, there's a lot of taking apart involved to get at and test the switch in most laptop designs. Fortunately, it's not a common failure.

Redo internal connections fix? Laptops get moved around, vibrated, bounced about and even flexed far more than desktop PC's. While laptop manufacturers use specially designed connectors, tape, and stress relievers to counter vibrations, it's not uncommon for connectors to work free. Find an illustrated guide that details how to open up your specific model of

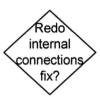

notebook (there's a lot of variations and tricks), take it apart, remake the connections, and put it back together again. If it works, but fails again at a later date, try to determine the exact connection that's failing by process of elimination. If you determine that a particular connection is prone to work itself loose, you can (out of warranty laptops only!) attempt to use an epoxy or mechanical restraint to hold it in place.

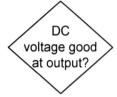

DC voltage good at output? The AC adapter for your laptop power supply transforms and rectifies AC to DC. The ratings for the DC output are printed on the label, 15V at 3.0 A, 19V at 2.0A, depends entirely on your model and the voltage of the battery used (the charging voltage has to be higher than the battery voltage). You can't play a mix and match game with AC adapters, it has to be the right voltage, supply enough current and have the exact barrel connector (inside and outside diameter and overall length) or it may cause damage or simply not work.

It's easy to check the voltage with an autoranging VOM, for non-autoranging meters, use the 20V range on the DC scale. While checking the voltage doesn't confirm that the transformer is supplying the required current, it's not as tricky as checking battery voltage where a surface charge can trick you into thinking a bad battery is good when no load is present. The voltage you read should be the same or a little higher than the voltages printed on the label. You can't confirm this by checking the DC plug with your tongue, and you may end up getting some spit in the connector that shorts out the whole works when you plug it back into the notebook. Be careful when one probe is inside the connector not to let it contact the probe on the outer conductor, or you'll short the AC adapter. Aside from the sparks, this could damage the AC adapter or the meter.

DC connector broken? The center pin of the DC barrel connector inside the laptop is a very common failure, sometimes breaking off altogether if the laptop is dropped while plugged in or if somebody trips over the cord. Note that some laptops are designed with the center pin as part of the AC adapter cord end. If the pin is missing but you're still getting intermittent power, it must be stuck inside the connector coming from the AC adapter and making contact with the broken part on the inside when it's plugged in tight. If the pin is loose to the touch, if it moves easily when you nudge it with a pencil point or a toothpick, it's probably hanging on by a thread and responsible for intermittent or limited power. The contact for the outside of the barrel can fail as well, especially if there are a limited number of solder points.

Replacing the connector inside the laptop, whether it's on the motherboard or on a special power regulation board, is one of the most labor intensive repairs a relative newbie can hope to carry out successfully. You need a lot of patience to disassemble the notebook to the point where you can desolder the old connector with a quality soldering iron with a fine tip. The connectors themselves can usually be found online for cheap, though an increasing number of laptops use proprietary connectors that can only be obtained from the manufacturer, who wants to sell you a whole new AC adapter if the cord fails. If you're very unlucky, the circuit board to which the connector is soldered may have broken in a drop, for which the only fix is replacing the whole board.

Power up no battery? If the laptop powers up with the battery removed, you've either got a bad battery or a problem with the connector in the battery compartment. Visually inspect the battery for damage and don't even try plugging it back in if it shows any signs of bulging, leaking or melting. Inspect the battery connector on the battery and in the battery compartment for signs of discoloration, misalignment or melted plastic on or near the pins. Some laptops won't operate without a battery installed, and any laptop that relies on the battery as part of the power supply conditioning circuit might be damaged by operation on poorly regulated power when the battery isn't installed. If the laptop does power up without the battery and the manufacturer or documentation confirms that battery-free operation is acceptable, you can treat it like a portable desktop. Otherwise, you can purchase a replacement battery, but the problem may turn out to be with the charging circuitry. Always check if your battery has been recalled before even thinking of purchasing a replacement.

Short or spark on DC jack? If you get a spark when you go to plug the DC output of the AC adapter into the laptop, remove it immediately and start looking for the short. Even if it doesn't spark, it's a logical step to check for a short circuit on the power input when you get no power LED on the laptop with a live AC adapter. If you have a dead AC adapter around, you can cut the

DC connector off, strip the two leads, and use the connector with the lead to test for a short with a meter set to continuity, or Ohms, if the meter lacks a continuity setting.

Assuming you don't have a spare lead, you can usually still check for a short without taking the laptop apart by measuring from the inner pin on the DC jack in the laptop to the metal on any of the laptop ports, which should be ground. If you have one of those odd laptops where the center conductor is ground, this will give a false indication, so make sure you check the polarity of the jack by testing the voltage coming from the AC adapter. You want the positive lead of the voltmeter (red) to contact the inside of the connector, and the ground (black) to contact the outside, and the readout to show the correct positive voltage. If it shows the voltage as negative, either the leads are plugged into the meter wrong or the DC connector carries the positive on the outside of the barrel.

The easier components to remove usually include the hard drive and the optical drive (DVD or CD), though it will be necessary to disassemble the laptop to remove them with some makes and models. Stripping the laptop down to its bare components is one step beyond simply disassembling and reassembling all in one step in an attempt to repair any faulty connections. If you keep your continuity meter connected by way of a spare lead or alligator clips on the inputs, you'll know the minute you solve the short. But if you insist on trying to find a short without a meter, it's best to strip the laptop down to nothing but the motherboard and video connections before trying to power it up again. Visually inspect the motherboard for damage before you apply the power.

If there's no short or sparks, the power problem in your laptop is likely related to an open circuit, due to a failed connection, broken trace or a burnt out component. One of the more common and easiest problems to diagnose at this point is a cold solder connection right at the DC input. It could be that the solder joints are physically sound enough so that the jack doesn't move around, but aren't conducting electricity, which you can check with a continuity meter or by measuring resistance on the Ohms scale. One of the connector conductors should be in continuity with any ground point in the laptop, or measure less than an Ohm, and the other conductor should have continuity to the circuit board trace for it, or to the positive leg of the next component the power reaches. If it's not a failed solder joint, check all of the components for visual signs of damage, reseat any daughter cards and connections, and try powering up again.

Live AC power source? You don't need a voltage meter to check for good AC power. Just unplug the AC adapter from the outlet it's in and plug in a lamp. If the lamp works, the power to the outlet is good, if not necessarily polarized correctly. Don't assume that because the light is flickering merrily away on a power strip that the power to the outlet you are plugged into on the strip is good, or that any of the outlets on the strip are good. Power strips have gotten so cheap that it's not uncommon to find multiple outlet failures on them.

DC voltage with connector cut off? If you've confirmed with a known good voltmeter set to the right scale that the DC connector on the AC adapter isn't putting out any voltage, you have nothing to lose by unplugging the AC adapter and cutting off the DC connector six inches or so before the connector end. Strip the end of the DC output cord still attached to the AC adapter, make sure the ends are separated when you plug the AC adapter back in, and check for DC voltage across the exposed ends. If there's no voltage, it's time to buy a new AC adapter. If the proper voltage is present, you'll need to buy a new connector and solder it onto the cord or make up a new connector with two leads and splice it onto the cord. You can order the connector ends online if you know exactly the size you need (may be shown in the manual for your laptop if you have it available or can find it online) but you can also bring the cut-off connector to a Radio Shack or electronics store and match it by eye if it's a basic, two conductor barrel connector.

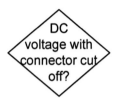

Laptop Won't Power Up With AC Adapter

Laptop Battery Failure

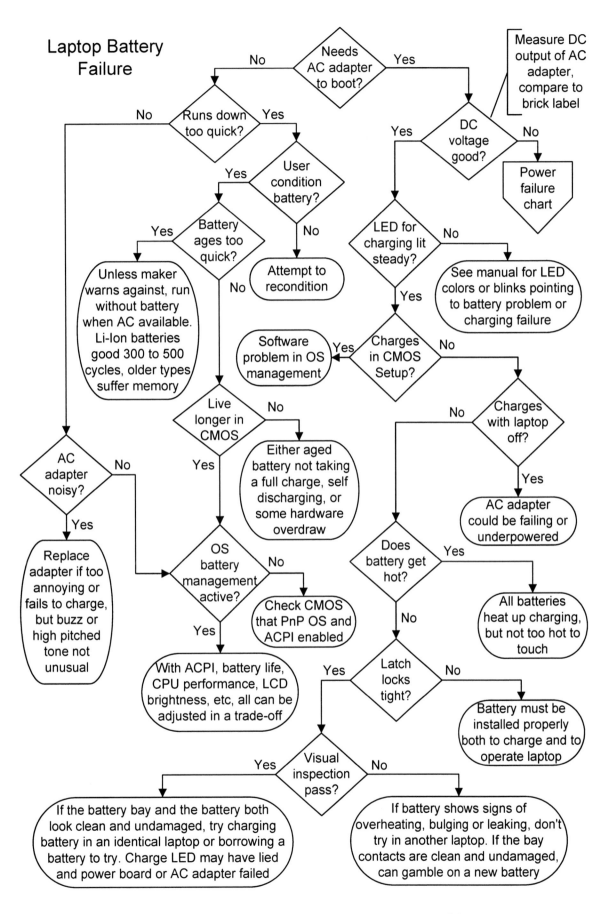

Needs AC adapter to boot?
- No → **Runs down too quick?**
- Yes → Measure DC output of AC adapter, compare to brick label → **DC voltage good?**

Runs down too quick?
- No → **AC adapter noisy?**
- Yes → **User condition battery?**

User condition battery?
- Yes → **Battery ages too quick?**
- No → Attempt to recondition

Battery ages too quick?
- Yes → Unless maker warns against, run without battery when AC available. Li-Ion batteries good 300 to 500 cycles, older types suffer memory
- No → **Live longer in CMOS**

DC voltage good?
- Yes → **LED for charging lit steady?**
- No → Power failure chart

LED for charging lit steady?
- No → See manual for LED colors or blinks pointing to battery problem or charging failure
- Yes → **Charges in CMOS Setup?**

Charges in CMOS Setup?
- Yes → Software problem in OS management
- No → **Charges with laptop off?**

Charges with laptop off?
- No → **Does battery get hot?**
- Yes → AC adapter could be failing or underpowered

Live longer in CMOS
- No → Either aged battery not taking a full charge, self discharging, or some hardware overdraw
- Yes → **OS battery management active?**

OS battery management active?
- No → Check CMOS that PnP OS and ACPI enabled
- Yes → With ACPI, battery life, CPU performance, LCD brightness, etc, all can be adjusted in a trade-off

AC adapter noisy?
- No → (to OS battery management active?)
- Yes → Replace adapter if too annoying or fails to charge, but buzz or high pitched tone not unusual

Does battery get hot?
- Yes → All batteries heat up charging, but not too hot to touch
- No → **Latch locks tight?**

Latch locks tight?
- Yes → **Visual inspection pass?**
- No → Battery must be installed properly both to charge and to operate laptop

Visual inspection pass?
- Yes → If the battery bay and the battery both look clean and undamaged, try charging battery in an identical laptop or borrowing a battery to try. Charge LED may have lied and power board or AC adapter failed
- No → If battery shows signs of overheating, bulging or leaking, don't try in another laptop. If the bay contacts are clean and undamaged, can gamble on a new battery

Needs AC Adapter to boot? The first step in troubleshooting your laptop battery is determining whether it can hold enough charge to boot the notebook. Will the laptop power up and run on the battery, or does the AC need to be plugged in all the time? Modern notebooks usually have a whole array of status LEDs that will tell you if the laptop senses good power coming from the AC adapter and whether or not the battery is charging. Unfortunately, there's no universal standard for these LEDs, their colors or their actions. Note also that we're using the term "boot" rather loosely here. If the laptop powers up on battery, you can hear the fans and the drives, but you don't get a live LCD, or fail to reach the operating system splash screen, you should start your troubleshooting with the LCD or hard drive.

Runs down too quick? This is the main problem laptop owners complain about, and often for good cause. Older laptops using Ni-Cad and early Ni-MH batteries ran for 2.5 to 3.5 hours when brand new, but often within a few short months could barely keep the notebook powered up for an hour. Newer laptops using Li-ion batteries are much better, normally holding onto a three or four hour life through hundreds of charge and discharge cycles. The first line of defense battery manufacturers employ against complaints about battery life is, "Did you charge and operate the battery according to the manual?" Unfortunately, different laptop manufacturers disagree over how to best treat batteries of the same technology, and some of the differences extend to various models from the same manufacturer.

Unless you have a very old laptop, the battery is actively monitored and managed by the operating system software. This means if there's an error in how the operating system sees the battery, whether due to hardware or software, you may get critical warnings and automatic shutdowns even if the battery isn't truly reaching a state of total discharge. One test for this is to temporarily change the action that accompanies the "critical battery alarm" in the battery management software from "hibernate" or "shut down" to "no action." If you get a critical warning, and then the laptop merrily works away for another two hours, you'll know the battery and the charger are working, but there's a software management problem. But you need to resolve the problem rather than just running that way or you'll risk losing work and possibly introducing data errors when the battery really does start running out of power and the system experiences a sudden brown-out.

User Condition Battery? Purchasers of brand-new laptops are often surprised to find the battery is dead, or runs down very quickly. Even if the battery was fully charged when the laptop was boxed for shipment, that box may have been sitting in a warehouse for six months or a year before you purchased it in a store. That's more than enough time for a notebook battery to self-discharge, even if it's not being drawn upon. If the battery isn't new, and you just received the laptop as a hand-me-down or purchased it second hand, there's no reason to expect that a short battery life is due to anything other than an aged battery. We strongly advise against trying any Internet inspired hacks for bypassing the built-in safety mechanism of Li-ion batteries unless you are a battery technologist yourself. The so-called "fuel gauges" or "odometers" that may prevent Li-ion batteries from accepting a charge after a fixed number of cycles are there to prevent overheating and fire risk as the battery's chemical composition changes with time.

Battery conditioning means training the individual battery cells into a pattern of giving as much power and accepting the largest charge that they can. It would take an advanced chemistry text and a much smarter author to describe the underlying reasons for battery memory, and the techniques for best charging and storing batteries sometimes contradict one another. Once a laptop battery pack is conditioned, you may still need to run it all the way down once a month for best performance, especially if you normally work with the laptop plugged in. It's important to read the owner's manual section on battery life, because different models ship with different battery technologies, and the best practices to extend the battery life may not be the same. You can try to recondition the battery (check the laptop manufacturer website for reconditioning software or instructions), but odds are the battery simply can't hold a charge the way it did when it was new.

Some manufacturers may condition the battery before installation in the laptop, others expect you to read the owner's manual instructions and do it yourself in the first few days you own the laptop. The most general procedure is to charge the battery fully before use (leaving it on the AC battery charger overnight is best), and then to run exclusively on battery until the battery is discharged. Some brands suggest you run until the operating system warns of low battery life remaining, which could be anywhere from 10% to 3% remaining, on standard settings. Others recommend that you run the laptop until it shuts itself down. This doesn't mean that you have to sit there working for three or four hours, you can run the battery down over multiple sessions over multiple days. The important thing is not to plug the AC power adapter back in and start recharging the battery until it is completely run down. The conditioning process may require you to go through this cycle three times in a row.

Battery ages too quick? If the laptop's battery life has been slowly degrading over time, it's probably operating more or less in accordance with plan, but if you find the operating life shortened by more than 20% or 25% within the first few months, there's likely something wrong. Ni-Cad and Ni-MH batteries can be "trained" to perform poorly through non-ideal usage patterns, and it usually helps if you run them all the way down once a month or so to prevent the worst charge memory issues. Some manufacturers of laptops using the new Li-ion technology encourage users to leave the batteries installed at all times, even if the laptop is almost always running on the AC adapter, while other manufacturers recommend removing the batteries and storing them somewhere cool when not needed for mobile use. Read your manual.

Live longer in CMOS? This is one of the few diagnostic tests for a battery you can do at home to find out if your battery life problem is due to hardware (the battery itself or the charging mechanism) or to the way the laptop is being operated. Enter CMOS setup immediately after turning on the notebook with a fully charged battery. Once you bring up the main CMOS Setup screen, start timing how long it takes the laptop battery to run down. If it doesn't outlast the battery life under regular usage by a good margin, the short battery life is probably due to a faulty battery or a hardware failure that causes the laptop to continually suck power when it shouldn't.

AC adapter noisy? This is one of those problems that tends to bother young women and children more than men, because men lose their high frequency hearing at an earlier age than women. AC adapters typically include a transformer and some power IC's, at least a bridge rectifier and some capacitors. There's a lot of potential for humming and whistling with transformers, but they can go on operating that way for years without failing. If the AC adapter gets burning hot as it whistles away, or starts to

smoke or smell, then pull the plug from the wall and buy a new one. In all cases, the acoustic behavior of your AC adapter may naturally vary with the quality of the power from the utility, and the feed voltage if you are traveling. Anytime you can avoid running a computer on poorly regulated or intermittent utility power you should do so, but at least the AC adapter offers a first line of defense against power spikes reaching the motherboard.

OS battery management active? Older notebooks were equipped with hardware only battery management schemes that controlled both charging and battery operation. All new laptops ship with ACPI (Advanced Configuration Power Interface) which is a marriage between BIOS routines that monitor board level charging and device activity, and the operating system. The operating system power management comes equipped with a number of default profiles that instruct the laptop if and how to nurse the battery. There's usually a power user profile that just runs full out with no consideration of battery life, a number of special purpose profiles, such as running a DVD movie for a sole task, and a miserly setting that cuts performance to a minimum and puts devices like the hard drive to sleep when not in frequent use.

You can micro-manage these profiles to suit your needs, and you can always go into the settings and override them or change the profile at any time. The most useful trick to remember for running on battery is how to brighten or dim the LCD screen using the function keys. Screen brightness is a serious power drain (you're essentially powering a bright fluorescent lamp) and in most indoor usage, strategic choice of where you sit can add time to your battery life. If you aren't working on the Internet, it also helps to turn off your wireless adapter when running on battery, and it's not a bad security practice either. Many laptops are equipped with an exterior switch to disable wireless, but you can do it in software as well. When troubleshooting battery life issues, you may want to run a power management profile for a few battery cycles that doesn't come up to your expectations for performance, just to help diagnose the problem.

If the battery management software reports errors or if the device driver for the battery is missing or in an error state, it could be due to an automated software update that went awry, or an inadvertent change to the CMOS settings. Enter CMOS

Setup and make sure that ACPI and PnP OS (Plug-n-Play operating system) are both enabled. If you can't find either of these options in Setup on a newer laptop, it probably means they are enabled by default. If the device driver for the battery remains in error state, check for an update on the manufacturer website, or consider going back to the last operating system restore point on Windows XP and later systems.

DC voltage good? Check the voltage at the output of your AC adapter with a DC voltmeter, right on the barrel connector that gets plugged into the laptop. We give a full explanation of DC voltage measurement and solutions in the text along with the power troubleshooting flowchart in the previous section. If you've purchased a lightweight battery charger for travel, don't assume that it's putting out the correct voltage just because there's a connector that fits your notebook. Check your owner's manual or the label on the original AC adapter that came with the notebook.

LED for charging lit steady? While there's no universal standard, a blinking LED on the battery charge indicator is probably not good news. It often indicates a battery that has been over-discharged, the voltage is so low that it's confusing the charging circuitry into thinking the battery has a dead cell and would just overheat if a charge is pushed into it. The newer the laptop, the smarter the charging logic, and it won't want to try putting a charge into a battery that may damage either the battery or the notebook itself. In some cases, you'll be able to recharge an over depleted battery if you wait until the notebook is shut down, install the battery, and then plug in AC adapter, and charge overnight without operating the laptop. There are also circuits built into some newer batteries that simply disable the battery when it reaches its planned cycle life.

The LED may tell you that it doesn't recognize that there's a battery present, which is a good time to jump ahead to the "Visual Inspection" steps on the flowchart to see if the problem is with the latching, mechanical contact or physical battery condition. Some models may even be able to differentiate between battery problems and a laptop charging problem, whether the battery charger regulation is included on the motherboard or on a daughter power board. But charging can always fail if the input from the AC adapter isn't sufficient, so always check the AC adapter before diagnosing an internal charging failure.

Charges in CMOS Setup? If the battery never charges when you're using your laptop, try entering CMOS Setup after powering up and letting the laptop sit on the Setup screen and charge for a few hours. If the battery does take a charge under these conditions, it means that the problem is likely with the operating system power management preventing the battery from charging. It's also remotely possible that your laptop usage when running is simply using all of the power provided by the AC adapter, so there's no current to spare for charging the battery.

Charges with laptop off? If your battery only takes a charge when you leave the AC adapter plugged in overnight and the laptop turned off, the problem is either with the BIOS level management of the battery or with the AC adapter. It's unlikely a laptop manufacturer would do such a bad job engineering their charging system, but it is possible if you've purchased a replacement AC adapter that is equipped with a variety of connectors and is intended to work with a large range of models. Some desktop replacement laptops have relatively high power requirements, and some very inexpensive laptops use less efficient components for cost savings.

Does battery get hot? Recently there have been a spate of high profile stories in the media about laptop batteries catching fire. This wasn't caused by normal heating due to charging. The problem was in the manufacturing process of the individual cells, where apparently some contamination led to internal short circuits that could cause the battery to overheat even if it wasn't in use. Laptop batteries normally heat up a little on charging, and they heat up even more when discharging under heavy demand. Battery packs include a temperature cut-off circuit, that will halt battery charging or discharging if it really overheats. In some cases, the battery will not be usable afterwards because the cut-off acts like a circuit breaker that can't be easily reset.

It certainly doesn't do your laptop battery any good to get very hot, even if it's within the toleration of the protective circuitry, so if it's overheating on discharge, consider running on AC power instead. Just remember you have to shut down before

100

removing the battery unless it's specified as being hot swappable. You can also try decreasing the performance settings to lower the power drain. If the battery is overheating on charging, you can try charging when the laptop is turned off since the laptop is generating heat as well. Also, pay attention to the ambient air temperature.

Latch locks tight? It's impossible to see what's going on with the connector contacts inside the battery compartment once the battery is installed, so the only indicator you have to proper installation (aside from normal operation) is the condition of the latch. If the latching mechanism doesn't show a positive close by clicking back to the relaxed position, try reinstalling the battery. Some laptops have a manual battery lock that is operating separately from the latches, and which will not lock unless the battery is installed properly. If the latches refuse to click closed on their own, remove the battery again, check for physical distortions in the battery package and damage to the connector both on the battery and in the bay.

Visual inspection pass? Always look before you leap into purchasing a replacement battery or swapping parts with an identical laptop. You don't want to damage a good laptop with your killer battery or waste your money on a new battery for your laptop if the connector in the bay is damaged beyond repair. Look for signs of discoloration on the surface of the battery, leakage, bulging, or opening seams. Any of these are a reason to safely dispose of the battery rather than trying it in another laptop. Likewise, if the battery looks physically perfect, but doesn't sit in the bay properly, there's a mechanical problem that may have been caused by dropping the laptop or overheating that will prevent any battery from fitting properly.

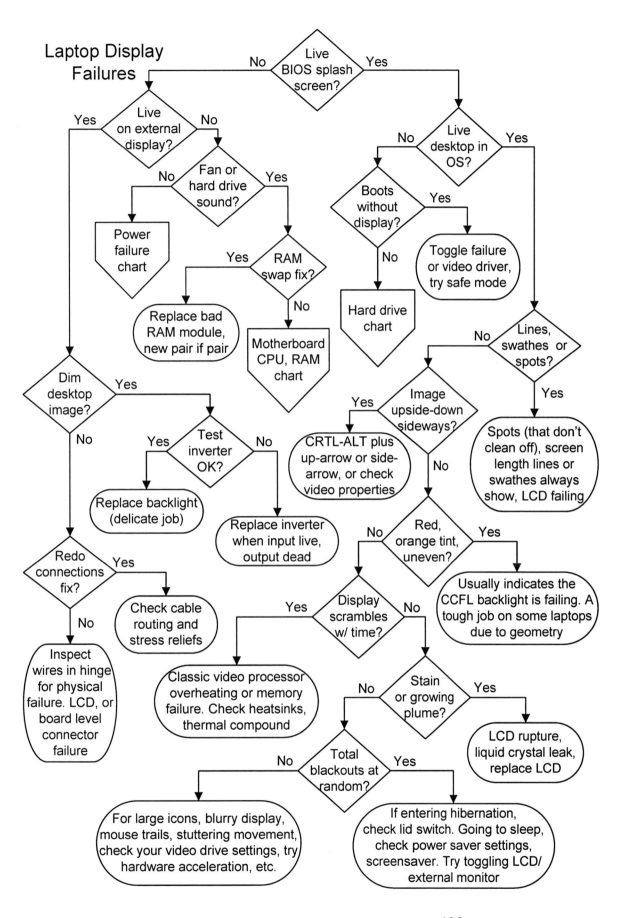

Laptop Display Failures

Live BIOS splash screen?
- No → Live on external display?
  - Yes → Dim desktop image?
  - No → Fan or hard drive sound?
    - No → Power failure chart
    - Yes → RAM swap fix?
      - Yes → Replace bad RAM module, new pair if pair
      - No → Motherboard CPU, RAM chart
- Yes → Live desktop in OS?
  - No → Boots without display?
    - Yes → Toggle failure or video driver, try safe mode
    - No → Hard drive chart
  - Yes → Lines, swathes or spots?

Dim desktop image?
- Yes → Test inverter OK?
  - Yes → Replace backlight (delicate job)
  - No → Replace inverter when input live, output dead
- No → Redo connections fix?
  - Yes → Check cable routing and stress reliefs
  - No → Inspect wires in hinge for physical failure. LCD, or board level connector failure

Lines, swathes or spots?
- No → Image upside-down sideways?
  - Yes → CRTL-ALT plus up-arrow or side-arrow, or check video properties
  - No → Red, orange tint, uneven?
    - No → Display scrambles w/ time?
      - Yes → Classic video processor overheating or memory failure. Check heatsinks, thermal compound
      - No → Stain or growing plume?
        - No → Total blackouts at random?
          - No → For large icons, blurry display, mouse trails, stuttering movement, check your video drive settings, try hardware acceleration, etc.
          - Yes → If entering hibernation, check lid switch. Going to sleep, check power saver settings, screensaver. Try toggling LCD/ external monitor
        - Yes → LCD rupture, liquid crystal leak, replace LCD
    - Yes → Usually indicates the CCFL backlight is failing. A tough job on some laptops due to geometry
- Yes → Spots (that don't clean off), screen length lines or swathes always show, LCD failing

Live BIOS splash screen? Most laptops will display a manufacturer splash screen with their brand name, Dell, Toshiba, Acer, Sony, etc, before launching into windows. Those that don't may flash a text screen with the BIOS maker (AMI, Award, Phoenix) in the corner, and a message telling you what key combination to use to access the BIOS Setup screens. A biometric screen prompting you to scan a fingerprint or an eyeball before the system will boot counts as a BIOS splash screen here. If the screen lights up with any graphic or text, it means that the basic display system is functioning. However, a pure white screen, or a series of color bars, does not count as a "live" screen here.

Live on external display? All notebooks should support an external monitor, usually with a high-density D-Shell 15 pin VGA connector, but some might feature a DVI connector also, or in place of VGA. It's a vital part of laptop display troubleshooting to determine if a known good external monitor can be used. Newer laptops don't keep the external connector live by default, and some don't allow for simultaneous display on both the LCD and an external monitor. Make sure you power down before attaching the external monitor, and on newer laptops, it may be detected on power up. Otherwise, you can toggle between the notebook screen (which isn't working) and the external display with an Fn key combination on most newer laptops, and a CTRL key combination on some older models. The Fn key is located at the lower left of the keyboard, normally between the CTRL and the ALT key. If you can't figure out the toggle combination by examining your keyboard symbols, try the user's manual or search on the web.

We'll list some of the more common models with recent toggles are here: Toshiba often uses Fn-F5 to toggle between the laptop LCD and an external display. IBM or Lenovo uses FN-F7, Acer varies with the model, using Fn-F5, Fn-F3, Fn-F8, Sony Fn-F7, Dell Fn-F8, HP or Compaq, Fn-F4. Apple PowerBooks and iBooks generally autosense external monitor connections, though you may choose the monitor icon on the Control Strip, or try a Command – F2 combination. Also, some Mac models have no external video port. There are variations with the age of the laptop and not all manufacturers have standardized on a key combo across the whole range, but you can usually figure it out from the little pictures on the function keys that line the top of the keyboard. If you read on the web that you need to enter

CMOS Setup to toggle to an external monitor, it isn't any help since you need to be able to read the screen to do it.

Fan or hard drive sound? If you can't get any life at all on the laptop LCD or the external display, it's entirely possible that the problem goes deeper than a video issue. Signs of life include the cooling fan blowing, the hard drive spinning up, any LED activity beyond the LED indicating AC power is attached or battery charging. If you don't see or hear any signs of life, proceed to power failure troubleshooting. If the system is powering up, even going through boot, you can often tell by the level of hard drive activity demonstrated by the sound or the hard drive LED flashing.

When the system does boot blind, with no signs of life on the LCD or external monitor, there aren't too many options. It could either be that you didn't successfully switch to the external monitor, that the output for the external monitor has failed or never worked and was simply never tried before, or that the video processor has failed in a manner undetectable by the BIOS. If the video failed while you were operating, or if it works briefly at boot time, it could be the video processor is overheating or has partially lost contact with the motherboard. It's worth searching the web to see if this is a problem endemic to your model. If the video processor is in a BGA (Ball Grid Array) package and is noted for a high failure rate of the solder connections in your model, you may be able to reflow the solder using a heat gun or other hack. If you are sure the system is truly booting blindly (you might put in a music CD and see if it auto-plays), you have a nearly working system.

RAM swap fix? Laptop video RAM is almost always shared with the system, so if the RAM has failed, the system won't boot and the video won't work. Not only is RAM failure one of the most common reasons for the laptop to fail to light up the screen or boot, it's also the easiest part in the laptop to replace, so it's always worth checking before digging further into the laptop guts and possibly creating new problems. If your laptop contains two RAM modules, or if you can borrow a compatible module from another laptop, you can check for failure without purchasing a new module. The RAM is accessed on most models by removing one or two screws from a panel on the bottom of the laptop. Unplug the AC adapter and remove the battery before proceeding. If you have two modules installed, remove the outer one, then try booting. If that doesn't work, swap the removed piece for the piece that's still installed and try again. If you have a compatible substitute module from another laptop or one that you purchased new, remove all of your installed RAM before trying it. Note that some old laptops had the base RAM soldered to the motherboard, and if it fails, it requires a board level repair you can't do at home.

Dim desktop image? Can you see a ghost-like image of your desktop that is functional, ie, one that changes if you drag an icon, launch a program or disappears if you shut down? Standard LCDs produce very little visible light on their own, they require the Cold Cathode Fluorescent Light (CCFL) to light the screen from behind. The fluorescent tube is normally located at the top of the screen, and a bright reflective surface distributes the light across the back of the LCD, so it can shine through the liquid crystals of the liquid crystal display, which only transmit red, green or blue (RGB). If you don't see a dim image, try holding a bright flashlight close to the screen at an angle, and see if you can make out the desktop.

Test inverter OK? Inverters put out high voltage, high frequency (something below the broadcast AM band) electrical signal, so you can't test them with the average handheld meter. If you have access to a higher quality RMS multi-meter, one that reads frequency into the KHz range, you may be able to test for inverter function without even taking the screen apart. The normal range for laptop inverters is between 30 KHz and 70 KHz, and meters will usually read signals well outside their specified range. A $20 meter rated for 20 KHz can probably pick up inverters operating up to 40 KHz, though it will just show a "1" for over-range if the inverter is active. A meter rated for 50 KHz should work for all inverters. If you can't pick up the field holding the probes against the plastic bezel, you can take the screen apart and try the probes on the insulated wires carrying the inverter output to the backlight. The test is to pick up the radiated electromagnetic field, so you never need to contact a bare conductor.

If you've already taken apart the screen, you can check the low voltage DC power into the inverter, which comes through a hinge from the motherboard. If the power to the inverter is good but there's no output, the inverter is bad, and can be usually be replaced for well under $100. If the output of the inverter is good and the backlight isn't lit, either the solder connections on the backlight have failed or the CCFL tube has failed. If you're the adventurous type and don't have access to a meter or a spare CCFL tube from another laptop, you can try a cheap CCFL tube from a PC modding kit, the $5 kind that are used to turn PCs into light shows. The tube won't be matched to the inverter, but if it lights up, the inverter is working. If the inverter starts smoking, it wasn't a good idea.

Redo connections fix? If taking the laptop apart and redoing all of the plug-together connections in the lid and the back of the LCD fixes the problem, you're golden. If not, inspect the wire harness running through the hinge to the lid for any signs of damage. It is still possible that you have a dead backlight or inverter and you can't see a dim image on the screen due to the type of LCD used, a darker than normal plastic film or less than perfect vision. Otherwise, you're faced with total LCD failure or a board level problem in the video subsystem output to the LCD, which is possibly a connector failure or a short in the cabling.

Live desktop in OS? After the operating system splash screen tells you what version of Windows or other OS you are using, does your usual desktop appear? If your sound is enabled and you usually get a "Windows rush" when you start the computer, you should hear it now. If the desktop does appear, the troubleshooting process shifts at this point to image quality and abnormalities.

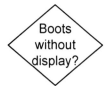

Boots without display? If the desktop never appears and you're left looking at a blank screen, but you can hear the hard drive is working away and other usual start-up sounds, or see the activity on the hard drive or wireless LEDs, the system is booting but the display isn't functioning. Another test is to put in an audio CD, and see if the drive spins up and the music starts playing, or checking if the keyboard is live by putting on Caps Lock and seeing if the LED lights. Try booting in Safe Mode, though if you shut down blind using the power switch, there's a good chance the laptop will start in Safe Mode by itself the next power-up. If you still can't get a live desktop, try attaching an external monitor, and if comes up fine, the problem is either an incompatible display resolution set in the operating system or a software setting forcing the OS to display on the external screen only after boot. See the notes about swapping under the troubleshooting symbol "Live on external display?"

If nothing you do gets a live desktop for even a moment, or if you don't hear any of the normal startup activity despite the live BIOS screen on power-up, the video subsystem is fine but the OS is failing to boot. The most likely reason for this is software corruption, including virus damage, or a physical problem with the hard drive. Proceed to hard drive troubleshooting.

Lines, swathes or spots? Assuming somebody didn't draw perfectly straight lines on your screen with a very thin magic marker or apply dots with the same, these are symptoms of physical LCD failure. It's not usually the liquid crystals that fail through rupturing, but the transistors that control their twist for individual pixels or address whole lines. The individual point failures may be tolerated if they aren't rapidly multiplying, They don't affect anything but your temper in terms of usability.

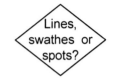

Laptop manufacturers normally specify some smallish number of dead pixels after which they will change the LCD under warranty. A pixel consists of three individual sub pixels of red, green and blue. When all are on together, the light mixes to produce white, when all are out, the result is black. The pixel failures don't have to be dead black spots, they can fail "on" as well, producing a white spot, or sub pixels can fail "on", meaning you'll always have a red, green or blue spot, which can be more annoying than black on a white desktop.

A whole swath of a solid color, black or white, usually indicates the failure of a chip (integrated circuit component) on the LCD that controls that range of horizontal or vertical lines on the screen. A large black (dead) bar all the way across or up and down the screen can also indicates that the ribbon connector is partially worked off the LCD panel or the motherboard. Cable connection failures are more common on certain laptop lemons where the connector was poorly designed and the cable is too short, so vibrations or flexing of the case tend to work it loose. If it's not a loose connection, and the display is affected by squeezing the edge of the lid, it's likely a contact on the edge of the LCD, which won't be repairable without replacing the whole LCD.

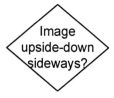

Image upside-down or backwards? Don't laugh if you already know the answer to this one, it's brought about more than one embarrassing service call for some hapless notebook owners. Many laptops have the ability to flip the display horizontally or vertically. You can do this from the keyboard, on purpose or accidentally, by hitting CTRL-ALT and the appropriate arrow from the direction arrows on the right-hand side of the keyboard. If the key combination doesn't do it, the problem is in software, either in the video driver properties or a malicious mirror program installed to make you wonky.

Red, orange tint, uneven? Is the entire screen tinted pink or orange (probably growing worse over time) or is the background brightness of the screen uneven, particularly near the edges? The tint is often caused by a failing backlight not putting out the full spectrum of white light, so the CCFL tube needs to be replaced. This can be a delicate job due to the latter problem, uneven lighting. The tube is very thin, flexible, and often installed underneath a reflective foil that wraps the whole back of the LCD panel. If the backlight tube is jolted or warped out of position, or if you install it poorly, you can end up with uneven lighting of the screen. You can live with it if you normally use an external monitor and only use the LCD on short jaunts out of the office, but otherwise, you'll need to try to correct the placement, which can be very difficult once the foil tabs are bent on some models. Some LCD panels are sold with integrated backlights that are nearly impossible to replace in the home setting.

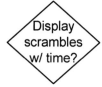

Display scrambles with time? This is the classic symptom of an overheating video processor or memory problems, assuming you aren't running a "dissolve" screensaver. Most laptops share main memory with the CPU, but memory modules don't have to fail all at once. See the text with the troubleshooting symbol in this section for "RAM swap fix." If you confirm that the RAM isn't the problem, you should check if the same thing happens with an external monitor before proceeding. If an external monitor works fine for hours without getting scrambled, the problem is likely with the electronics on the LCD panel.

But if the problem appears on both the laptop LCD and an external monitor and it's not the RAM, the prime suspect remaining is the video processor. A video processor may also display these symptoms if the entire laptop is running too hot, due to failure of the main cooling fan, clogging or obstruction of the intake or exhaust vents. Make sure you are running the laptop on a flat surface, with some open space to all sides, and if overheating is suspected, proceed to the section on troubleshooting overheating. The problem may clear up when you run in a power saver mode on battery with the processing speed turned down. You can also try turning off hardware acceleration in the advanced properties of the video adapter in the operating system.

If all else fails and the problem is specific to the video processor, your best bet is opening up the body of the notebook and reinstalling the heatsink on the video processor. Search the Internet first to find illustrated instructions for your exact model. Make sure there is enough thermal compound (or not too much!) and if equipped with a fan, that the fan is still turning. While you're on the Internet, research video problems with your model and if the video processor is a soldered BGA (Ball Grid Array) chip, see if it's a common failure for your system. There are several solder reflow hacks that may cure your system, at least temporarily, but they are really intended for users with advanced technical skills. Reflowing solder with a heat gun requires removing the motherboard, stripping it down to nothing and covering vulnerable areas with tin foil. You can find some video presentations of the technique on YouTube.

Stain or growing plume? If a blotch appears on the LCD that isn't due to food on the screen or dirty fingerprints, and it grows over time, it's the physical failure of the glass sandwich and can't be repaired. This might also appear like octopus ink being slowly injected into the screen, a sort of growing plume. The only cure is replacing the LCD.

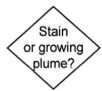

Total blackouts at random? One possible cause of seemingly random, total blackouts, is a loose connection. However, before you take the body and the lid of the laptop apart and remake all of the connectors in the video subsystem, it's worth checking the more obvious culprits, like a screen saver set to "blank" and poor wake-up behavior, or the video getting toggled to a non-existent external monitor by a keyboard failure (or operator failure). Check the power saver settings as well, and try running on a different power profile for a while in case the one you have been using is corrupt. Likewise, try running on battery in a low power mode to see if the blackouts are an overheating issue, but that's

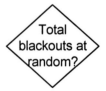

unlikely if the screen returns to the point you left off with some judicious tapping or moving of the lid.

If the problem is unfamiliar distortions to the display, such as multiple screens displayed, only part of the desktop visible or a very blurry image, these are all signs of the video resolution having been changed to a bad choice, one which doesn't match the native resolution of the LCD. Change the video properties in the operating system back to native resolution of the LCD, usually the highest resolution and number of colors offered. If the problem is large icons or a change in font size, this is due to display property choices in the operating system or in the particular application showing the symptoms.

Laptop Overheating

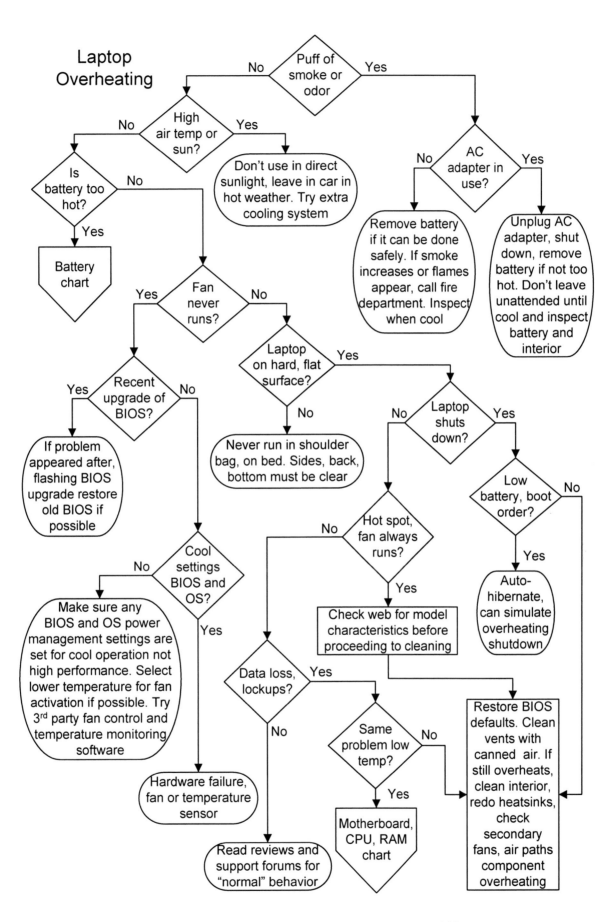

Puff of smoke or odor

No — High air temp or sun?

Yes — Don't use in direct sunlight, leave in car in hot weather. Try extra cooling system

No — Is battery too hot?

Yes — Battery chart

No — Fan never runs?

Yes — Recent upgrade of BIOS?

Yes — If problem appeared after, flashing BIOS upgrade restore old BIOS if possible

No — Cool settings BIOS and OS?

No — Make sure any BIOS and OS power management settings are set for cool operation not high performance. Select lower temperature for fan activation if possible. Try 3rd party fan control and temperature monitoring software

Yes — Hardware failure, fan or temperature sensor

No (Fan never runs?) — Laptop on hard, flat surface?

No — Never run in shoulder bag, on bed. Sides, back, bottom must be clear

Yes — Laptop shuts down?

No — Hot spot, fan always runs?

No — Data loss, lockups?

Yes — Check web for model characteristics before proceeding to cleaning

Yes (Hot spot, fan always runs?) — Check web for model characteristics before proceeding to cleaning

Yes (Data loss, lockups?) — Same problem low temp?

No — Read reviews and support forums for "normal" behavior

No (Same problem low temp?) — Restore BIOS defaults. Clean vents with canned air. If still overheats, clean interior, redo heatsinks, check secondary fans, air paths component overheating

Yes — Motherboard, CPU, RAM chart

Yes (Laptop shuts down?) — Low battery, boot order?

Yes — Auto-hibernate, can simulate overheating shutdown

No — Restore BIOS defaults. Clean vents with canned air. If still overheats, clean interior, redo heatsinks, check secondary fans, air paths component overheating

Puff of smoke or odor — Yes — AC adapter in use?

No — Remove battery if it can be done safely. If smoke increases or flames appear, call fire department. Inspect when cool

Yes — Unplug AC adapter, shut down, remove battery if not too hot. Don't leave unattended until cool and inspect battery and interior

Puff of smoke or odor? Never play with fire. If you see smoke or smell a burning odor, it's not something you can afford to ignore. In some instances, brand new laptops will give off a bit of odor when they are first powered on that smells a little like hot plastic and a little like the ocean. In any other situation, smoke or smells coming from your laptop are not normal. If you recently spilled something on the laptop and have already dried it out and cleaned it to the best of your ability (or your repair person's ability), there may be a little residual burning off the first time you run the laptop and get it up to operating temperature.

Burnt odors are usually from overheated plastic component packages out-gassing, and where there's smoke there may be fire. If the problem is in any way associated with a hot Li-ion battery, put the thing outdoors if you can safely do so. Whether or not a particular manufacturer issued a recall for the battery in your laptop, a manufacturing flaw in a Li-ion cell can lead to fire. Even if the puff of smoke isn't repeated or the odor goes away as soon as the laptop cools down, you should make a serious effort to locate the component at fault rather than just powering up again and hoping for the best.

High air temp or sun? All laptops will overheat if you use them in a cruel enough environment. Obvious examples are stifling hot attics, vehicles without air conditioning in the summer or on hot surfaces. Hot surfaces aren't limited to radiators or metal desks touching steam pipes, they also include dark surfaces that get a lot of direct sunlight, even if they are located indoors. Using a laptop outside in direct sunlight in the summer is more than a problem for your eyes, especially if the laptop case is dark rather than reflective. Always remember that laptop computers are entirely reliant on air flow for cooling, and the higher the ambient air temperature, the less the laptop will be able to cool itself.

Is battery too hot? Some people are more sensitive to temperature than others, so using "too hot to touch" isn't a great troubleshooting technique. Unfortunately, very few people have a thermometer around capable of measuring temperatures through the normal operation range of a battery, including most computer technicians, so touch is all most people will have to go on. If the battery seems excessively hot, check the web to see if it's been included in a recall or if a hot battery is typical of the particular laptop model. Then proceed to the battery troubleshooting flowchart.

Fan never runs? Most laptop users are accustomed to hearing the cooling fan(s) straining away during certain intensive computing operations, and even the quietest, best behaved notebooks normally cycle the fan on and off at low RPMs during normal operation. If the fan never runs, it doesn't mean your laptop is overheating, but it could mean that something may be wrong with the fan or the settings. If something is wrong with the fan or the temperature controller, eventually the laptop will overheat, unless you do all of your work in a walk in freezer.

Recent upgrade of BIOS? Anecdotally speaking, it seems that "my fan never comes on anymore" problems often occur after a BIOS upgrade. Manufacturers generally encourage users to install the latest BIOS version available for the model on the manufacturer's website, and if you call tech support with an in-warranty overheating problem, the first thing they are likely to do is tell you to upgrade to the latest BIOS. The problem is, the notebook really should operate normally with the BIOS version you purchased it with, or they shouldn't have sold it to you. If you want to add new peripherals or upgrade an internal component and it's not supported unless you upgrade the BIOS, you don't have much choice. Outside of that, avoid BIOS upgrades like the plague, keeping in mind that a failed upgrade can leave you with a paperweight that can only be repaired by sending it out. If the fan problem appeared after you upgraded the BIOS and the laptop which was operating fine originally is now overheating, try reinstalling the original BIOS if it's available.

Cool settings BIOS and OS? There's no universal standard for what BIOS settings are user adjustable for a given brand or model of laptop. If you're having overheating problems and you can lower the temperature at which the fan automatically powers up, it can't hurt to do so. There are a large number of operating system settings that affect the amount of heat the laptop will generate, from the speed of the processor and the brightness of the screen to the settings for cooling efficiency. The manufacturers try to give the user as much control as possible, so if you or another user ran the cooling control down to the minimum to reduce fan noise while listening to Internet radio, it may be time to compromise.

If the settings are all on the defaults, the fan never comes on, and the system is overheating, it's either a fan failure or a problem with the control circuit. The fan itself is a replaceable DC fan that can often be replaced without removing the heatsink (if it's mounted directly on the CPU or graphics processor). One simple test for notebook fans is to gently blow on them. If the fan doesn't spin, either the bearing has failed or something is melted or jammed, because the motors are tiny. Testing the control circuit is an open-unit bench job for experienced technicians. It's easier and less time consuming to just replace the fan with a known good unit, and if it still doesn't work the problem is in the controller or the power supply to the fan. Replacement fans are sold by size, measured in millimeters, giving the length, width (normally the same since they're square) and height. Don't buy a fan online without seeing a picture of it so you can determine if it matches your mounting hardware. Fans are sold with a two pin connector or with bare leads for soldering.

Laptop on hard, flat surface? The leading cause of laptop overheating is what engineers call "poor siting." Notebook computers are designed to run on flat level surfaces, with at least a couple inches of unobstructed space all around. Running a laptop computer sitting in the opened shoulder bag on your lap is a great way to block intake and exhaust vents and overheat the poor computer. Running on a bed is equally bad for laptops that have vents on the bottom, and if it's a soft bed or there are loose sheets and blankets, the side vents can get blocked as well. Running on your lap is generally discouraged by manufacturers, but most laptops do get run on a lap from time to time. Be sure to locate and avoid blocking any air vents on the bottom. If you're troubleshooting an intermittent laptop overheating problem, the first check is to pick a nice cool place with a large flat surface to run the notebook and see if the problem clears up.

Laptop shuts down? Computers may not be smarter than people, but if they're designed properly, they will shut themselves down before overheating to the extent that they do themselves damage. If the smart person keeps turning the notebook back on and figures out a way to foil the protection, the laptop is probably doomed. Once a laptop shuts down for thermal event protection, it may refuse to power back up for a few minutes, or it may begin to boot and shut down as soon as it gets to the point that it can figure out that it's too hot.

The over-temperature protection is generally a BIOS rather than an operating system function. One sure sign of an overheated laptop is one that shuts itself down while you're using it and then refuses to boot as far as the operating system unless you leave it alone for an hour or so to cool down. Unless you've been working temporarily in a very unfriendly environment, with high temperatures, direct sunlight, etc, you should take even a single overheating shutdown as a warning to back up your data at the first opportunity. If you can't keep your laptop from shutting down long enough to do a back-up, some people have reported success starting the process and putting the whole laptop in the fridge until it's complete.

Hot spot, fan always runs? Many laptop brands and models have characteristic hot spots, like a particular corner of the keyboard or above the battery compartment. Before proceeding with the more invasive cleaning techniques that involve opening up the laptop (and potentially breaking something), spend some time searching the web for user feedback on your make and model. The bothersome hot spot on your laptop that none of your friends or colleagues have ever heard of may be a characteristic issue with your particular model and not worth a major panic. Similarly, if the fan always runs, or almost always runs, it may be a characteristic of the particular model that it simply gets hot in normal operation, or the fan control software might be poorly conceived. As long as the laptop isn't overheating and the fan behavior is typical for the model, you should learn to live with it and only get worried when you don't hear it anymore.

Data loss, lockups? Troubleshooting all of the software problems that can cause data loss is beyond the scope of page sized flowcharts. Overheating of the CPU, the RAM or the hard drive can cause data corruption and lead to the laptop locking up, but overheating is only one of many potential culprits. If you haven't noticed any change in fan noise or any increase in the heat you sense from the laptop, it's possible that the problems are due to another cause. See the hard drive and motherboard, CPU and RAM troubleshooting flowcharts.

Same problem low temperature? Wait until the laptop is completely cooled down (overnight), use it in a cool or air conditioned environment and find out if the errors you were encountering repeat soon after you boot. If the errors do repeat and the problem was related to overheating, the damage is already done and you now have a hardware failure problem. Checking the other flowchart for motherboard, CPU and RAM troubleshooting may narrow down the problem. If the problems don't immediately come back when the laptop is first booted cold, but only appear once it heats up, it's possible that a thorough cleaning and inspection will help clear up the problem that's causing the overheating, and no hardware replacement will be necessary.

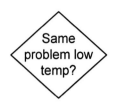

Low battery, boot order? The default setting for most laptops when they reach a critically low battery state is to go into hibernation, the quickest way they can save any data in open applications and drop into a lower power state until the AC adapter is connected. If the battery has failed and won't accept a charge, if there's a problem with the AC adapter, or if the operating system software isn't as clever as it should be, the system may get locked into a loop. As soon as the operating system boots to the point where it can identify a battery problem, it goes back into hibernation waiting for salvation. In some rare instances the laptop may continue this looping behavior with the battery removed. If the battery and AC adapter are good, the slow fix is to let it charge overnight before trying to boot. If that doesn't work, try changing the boot order in the CMOS Setup to the CD/DVD, just to break the loop.

Cleaning process. Do the simple things first. Close the laptop lid, unplug all cords, inspect all four edges and the bottom of the laptop for air vents to familiarize yourself with where they are. If you spot air vents on the bottom about where you are accustomed to holding it on your thighs, that's probably the whole problem right there. Likewise, some people misunderstand the concept of creating more air clearance under the laptop and try jacking it in the air an inch with a book. If the book is smaller than the laptop, it will likely fit between the little legs or pads on the bottom of the laptop that are there to raise it off the table for air circulation, and it will overheat even faster than before.

Restore BIOS defaults. Clean vents with canned air. If still overheats, clean interior, redo heatsinks, check secondary fans, air paths component overheating

As you look into the vents, you may see dust build-up on foil radiators or heatsinks, not to mention on the fan assembly if it is visible. Depending on the size of the vents, you may be able to loosen up and capture some of the dust with Q-tips (cotton swabs). The problem with using compressed air to clean a laptop without taking it apart is that while you'll definitely blow the dust off wherever you aim the air stream, you'll often be blowing it somewhere else in the notebook. The immediate result will be a cooler running notebook because you've removed the dust and lint build-up on heatsinks which can act as a blanket and keep the heat from being radiated and conducted away. But if all you've accomplished if throwing that blanket over some other hot components that aren't visible through the vents, you may have greater problems in the future. Make sure you use a can of compressed air sold for cleaning electronics, otherwise there may be harmful propellants or liquids mixed in. Read the instructions, and if they tell you to always hold the can upside up, be careful to obey. Holding it upside down may result in squirting propellant rather than compressed air.

Before opening up the laptop, find the owner's manual or search the web for exact instructions. Once you gain access to the active cooling components, fans and heatsinks, you can blow off all the dust with compressed air and get most of it out of the case. Some fans may be damaged if you spin them up beyond their operating RPMs with the compressed air, so you should prevent the fan from spinning if blasting it up close. Pay careful attention to the air paths in the laptop and look for any blockages, both when you open it up and when you go to put it back together. Notebooks are generally engineered with very little slack in the cables to keep them from flopping around and potentially breaking up the airflow, but something as innocuous as a loose paper label flipping up and blocking an air path can cause a world of trouble.

In severe cases of laptop overheating, especially those where data corruption or automatic shutdowns are occurring, you should check that any heatsinks are properly installed. The only way to do this is to remove them. Depending on the design of the laptop, you may have active heatsinks on both the CPU and the video processor, and there may be some passive heatsinks with fans strategically located to circulate air over them. Some passive heatsinks are basically glued to the package and can't be removed. If you try pulling on them, you could damage the component or the motherboard. The active heatsinks are normally mounted with a latching mechanism or screws and can be removed, though they might stick pretty fiercely to the processor depending on the condition of the existing thermal paste.

When you purchase the new thermal paste, it may be sold in a kit with a thermal paste cleaner. Cleaning up the old goo is just as important as applying the new goo properly. Don't use household cleaners to clean up thermal paste, they can leave an oily residue that actually prevents heat from conducting to the active heatsink, worse than nothing. If you don't purchase a cleaning kit, the fallback is scraping with a credit card and cleaning with isopropyl (rubbing) alcohol on a clean cloth or paper towel. Once the new paste is applied and you've reinstalled the active heatsink and closed up the case, there's no guarantee that your overheating problem will be solved. Overheating may be a symptom of chip level degradation and imminent failure. While poor cooling was likely a contributing factor, closing the barn door after the cow is gone isn't going to undo the damage.

AC adapter in use? If you see a puff of smoke or smell a burning odor and the AC adapter is in use, you should unplug it immediately if you can. You can burn your fingers or even electrocute yourself on the AC side of the cord, so exercise extreme caution. When there's a risk of fire, as documented in laptops with defective batteries, your first priority should be guarding against an outbreak of fire, not worrying about the laptop condition or studying this flowchart. Some people will immediately call the fire department or grab the fire extinguisher at the first sign of smoke in electronics. If there are flames coming out of the laptop, it's history, so the fire extinguisher or fire department is the way to go. If it's just a puff of smoke, the action may all be over and unplugging the AC may preserve a laptop that can be reasonably repaired.

Troubleshooting the cause of the smoke, unless you just poured your coffee on the keyboard, requires taking the laptop apart and visually inspecting the components down to the board level. If the laptop is at all hot, wait for it to cool before attempting disassembly. Always remove the battery pack before opening up a laptop. Since component spacing in laptops is so tight, you'll rarely get lucky enough to zero in on the problem with your sense of smell, which is sometimes effective with larger desktop computer components.

Inspect the circuit boards, connectors, remove and inspect the drives. Pay special attention to electrolytic capacitors and discrete power semiconductors, usually located very near the power input. If you find a burnt spot or signs of melting on a discrete component, such as a hard drive, DVD drive, capacitor or power semiconductor, there's a reasonable chance that the failure was internal to that component and that replacing it will fix the problem. If there's a large burnt or melted spot on the motherboard, it's rarely cost effective to even attempt a replacement.

If the problem was a hot plastic odor and you can't find any signs of damage during your visual inspection, it's possible that the laptop was overheating and you caught it in time. Some people are more sensitive than others to plastic odors, and there is always the possibility that a little foreign matter, food or insect, found its way into the laptop and got incinerated. Read over the procedures for troubleshooting laptop overheating, as if you never encountered the burnt odor, and make sure the notebook wasn't operated in such a way that it was being encouraged to overheat.

Laptop Drive Problems

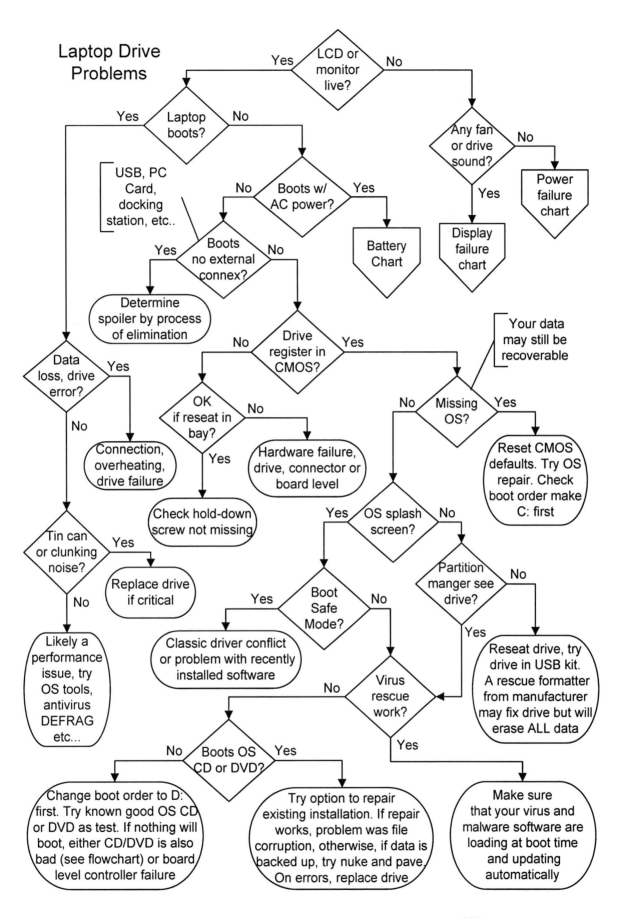

LCD or monitor live?
- Yes → **Laptop boots?**
- No → **Any fan or drive sound?**
  - No → Power failure chart
  - Yes → Display failure chart

Laptop boots?
- Yes → USB, PC Card, docking station, etc.. → **Data loss, drive error?**
- No → **Boots w/ AC power?**

Boots w/ AC power?
- No → **Boots no external connex?**
- Yes → Battery Chart

Boots no external connex?
- Yes → Determine spoiler by process of elimination
- No → **Drive register in CMOS?**

Drive register in CMOS?
- No → **OK if reseat in bay?**
- Yes → **Missing OS?** (Your data may still be recoverable)

OK if reseat in bay?
- No → Hardware failure, drive, connector or board level
- Yes → Check hold-down screw not missing

Missing OS?
- No → **OS splash screen?**
- Yes → Reset CMOS defaults. Try OS repair. Check boot order make C: first

Data loss, drive error?
- Yes → Connection, overheating, drive failure
- No → **Tin can or clunking noise?**

Tin can or clunking noise?
- Yes → Replace drive if critical
- No → Likely a performance issue, try OS tools, antivirus DEFRAG etc...

OS splash screen?
- Yes → **Boot Safe Mode?**
- No → **Partition manger see drive?**

Partition manger see drive?
- Yes → **Virus rescue work?**
- No → Reseat drive, try drive in USB kit. A rescue formatter from manufacturer may fix drive but will erase ALL data

Boot Safe Mode?
- Yes → Classic driver conflict or problem with recently installed software
- No → **Virus rescue work?**

Virus rescue work?
- No → **Boots OS CD or DVD?**
- Yes → Make sure that your virus and malware software are loading at boot time and updating automatically

Boots OS CD or DVD?
- No → Change boot order to D: first. Try known good OS CD or DVD as test. If nothing will boot, either CD/DVD is also bad (see flowchart) or board level controller failure
- Yes → Try option to repair existing installation. If repair works, problem was file corruption, otherwise, if data is backed up, try nuke and pave. On errors, replace drive

123

Laptop Drive Problems

LCD or monitor live? The first step in troubleshooting hard drive problems is determining whether or not you are dealing with a hard drive failure or something else entirely. If neither your LCD screen nor an external monitor show any signs of intelligent life from the laptop when it's powered on, the problem will rarely be related to the hard drive.

Laptop boots? Does the laptop start up normally, get you all the way to the desktop? If the laptop boots, unless you are dealing with a noise issue, the problem you're having is either software related or an accumulation of errors on the drive. If the laptop doesn't boot, we'll move on to troubleshooting why it doesn't boot before blaming the hard drive.

Data loss, drive errors? If the operating system disk maintenance software, such as ScanDisk, is reporting errors every time you run it, if you see text messages about "write failures" or if successive surface scans report a large number of errors, your hard drive is actually failing. Before you conclude that the hard drive needs replacing, make sure that you aren't operating the laptop in an environment it wasn't designed for. Overheating can lead to hard drive recording errors, as can taking it up to 20,000 feet in an observation balloon, or excessive vibrations from operating on public transportation systems. It's also possible that the hard drive data connector is barely making contact with a couple of pins, so reseat the drive and make sure it's secured properly in the bay before giving up on it.

Tin can or clunking noises? If your laptop hard drive develops new noises over time, if it sounds like a motor in a tin can or starts making frequent clunking noises, it may be a sign of impending failure. If you have important data, you should start backing up more frequently, and if you use the laptop for critical work and want to minimize the chances of it failing when you most need it, you can replace the hard drive at this point. However, hard drive noise can go on for years and years, and no doubt more people throw away working laptops with noisy hard drives than throw away laptops due to hard drive failure.

If you're getting very flaky errors, having difficulty when connected to the Internet, are seeing large scale file corruption or data loss, the problem is more likely due to malware (bad software such as a computer virus, spyware, trojans) than electronic or mechanical failure. Another cause for data corruption is letting the amount of free space on the drive fall so low that the operating system has trouble managing virtual memory. The old rule of thumb was to keep about 10% of the drive free, and even though drives are much bigger these days, the amounts of data held in RAM have grown as well. It's also critical to have free space available when you run system tools to optimize hard drive performance, like a defragmentation program.

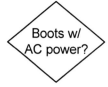

Boots with AC power? If the laptop boots up with the AC power adapter plugged in, the problem is with the battery, not the hard drive. Proceed to the battery troubleshooting flowchart. If you notice the hard drive performance seems to degrade badly when you are running on battery power, it means the power management is turning off the hard drive after too short of a delay on no activity, probably just a minute or two. You can change the power management setting to increase the shut-down delay for the hard drive or to ensure the hard drive remains spun up as long as the laptop is turned on.

Boots no external connex? If you have any external devices plugged into your notebook, such as printers, cameras, PC Cards (the replacement for PCMCIA cards), external keyboards or mice, network cables, monitors, unplug them all. If the laptop is sitting in a docking station, remove it. If the laptop boots when all of the external connections are removed, the problem isn't the hard drive, it's a faulty external device or signal. You can determine which device is preventing the OS from booting by process of elimination. The problem isn't necessarily a hardware failure, it could be the driver for that device is so unfriendly or corrupted that it's stalling the boot process when called to manage its client.

Drive register in CMOS? Does the laptop BIOS see that a hard drive is installed and correctly identify it in CMOS Setup? If not, try restoring the BIOS defaults or "Safe Settings" in case the CMOS settings have been corrupted. If the BIOS still doesn't register the hard drive, either the hard drive has failed, the connector has failed or come undone, or you have a board level problem. Don't jump to flashing the BIOS because the hard drive doesn't show up, unless it's a replacement drive and the previous hard drive still registers if you reinstall it. The original hard drive should always be recognized by the existing BIOS if the hardware is in operating condition and the connector hasn't come undone. If reseating the hard drive fixes the problem, make sure that it isn't missing a hold down screw.

Missing OS? If the BIOS reports "Missing OS" or "OS not found" during the boot process and you just installed a brand new hard drive, it just means you still have to install the operating system. Next check the boot order in the BIOS, make sure the C: is the first boot device and restore the BIOS defaults. Otherwise, you could have a hardware failure, but it's far more likely that the operating system has been corrupted. While file corruption can occur for non-fatal reasons, such as glitches during overheating or vibration and shock, the leading cause is probably computer viruses or operator error, writing over or deleting required system files. If you have a rescue disk generated by your virus protection software, try running it, after which you can boot the OS CD/DVD (if you have one) and try a repair installation, if necessary. But keep a close eye on the prompts, and if you're told that proceeding will wipe out all the data and programs on your hard drive, stop if you aren't willing to lose them.

OS splash screen? Does the operating system load get as far as the splash screen, which will be the Windows flag on most laptops? If it does, odds are that your drive is largely intact and the data should be recoverable even if you can't get back to your previous operating state with the tools you have available. If the splash screen doesn't show and hard drive contains essential information that hasn't been backed up, it's a good time to consider calling in a professional for data recovery. While the problem may not prove to be serious, your attempts to get the laptop back to a bootable state may end up making the data recovery job harder, more expensive, or even impossible.

Boot Safe Mode? If the laptop will boot up in Safe Mode, it's usually in pretty good shape but is having a problem with a recently installed (or recently corrupted) piece of software or device driver. If the boot failure has occurred immediately after installing a new program or peripheral and restarting, the first step is to uninstall the software that was just installed, or disconnect the new peripheral and remove the driver before attempting to reboot. In some instances, simply starting in Safe Mode will allow Windows to recover it's equilibrium and the system will boot normally as soon as you shut down properly and restart.

Partition manager see drive? All operating system install discs ship with a partition manager, even if it's a version of the old FDISK. Some new hard drives sold in retail packages also ship with manufacturer provided partitioning software. If whatever partition manager software you have doesn't see the hard drive, it's either a hardware failure or the MBR (Master Boot Record) has been corrupted. Before you do anything else, try reseating the hard drive in the laptop. If that doesn't work, consider buying a USB enclosure that will allow you to try to read and recover the hard drive data on another computer. If all else fails and you don't care about recovering the data, you can try running the factory formatter at this point if they provide one on their website, but it will destroy all data on the drive.

Virus rescue work? If you installed virus protection software or a full protection suite on the laptop, you were probably given the option to create a bootable rescue DVD or CD (rescue floppies went out the window with floppy drives). If you created a rescue disc, this is a good time to try it. If the rescue CD restores your operating system to a bootable condition, it could be that you had automatic updates turned off and you've been running with out-of-date virus definitions. Make sure that you are receiving daily updates to your virus and spyware protection software. It could also be indicative of file corruption caused by overheating or the usual run of hard drive or motherboard issues.

Boots OS CD or DVD? If you can boot the operating system or factory restore disc that the notebook was sold with, you can try doing a repair installation, which should leave your file system and your data intact. Just don't agree to any prompts which inform you that your data will be wiped out if you proceed. Booting the OS CD with a JumpDrive in the USB port may get you command prompt access to the JumpDrive, so you can back up critical data if you haven't done so already. If the repair installation works, the problem was file corruption, or accidental deletion of necessary files. If you don't need the data or programs on the drive or you have them backed up, you can try the nuke and pave option, telling either the operating system or the factory restore software to do a new installation. In extreme cases of corruption, you may need to manually use the partitioning software to delete the primary partition and then letting the OS install disc do its thing on the next boot. This will result in wiping out all data and any programs you installed.

If you can't get the OS or factory restore disc to boot, try changing the boot order so that the D: drive is the first boot device. If that doesn't work, make sure you have a good boot CD or DVD by trying it in another computer, or getting one that works in another computer. Don't assume that the disc that shipped with your laptop is bootable or good, even if it's in the original packaging and you never used it. Some manufacturer rescue discs require you turn on the laptop with a particular key held down, or hit a key combination when the screen lights up. You'll have to check the Internet for your particular model to see if this is necessary, though instructions are often written on the envelope the disc is packed in. If you can't get an OS to boot in the CD/DVD drive no matter what you try, the drive may be bad or you could have a board level controller failure affecting both drives. See the troubleshooting chart for CD/DVD failure.

Any fan or drive sound? If you don't hear anything at all when you try to turn the laptop on, no little LED's light up, the problem is rarely related to the hard drive. So if you don't have a live screen, start with the LCD troubleshooting flowchart, and if you don't have any activity at all, start with the power troubleshooting flowchart. Even if the hard drive has failed at the electro/mechanical level and won't spin up, this won't prevent the LED's on the laptop from lighting up, or the LCD from displaying the BIOS information and complaining about the lack of a boot device.

Laptop Internet Connectivity

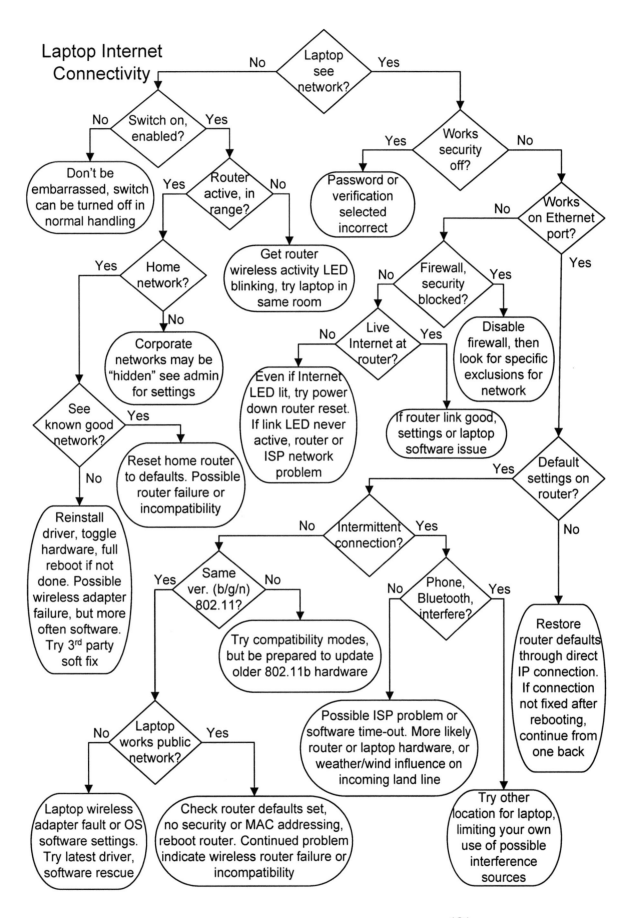

Laptop see network? Does the laptop operating system software see the wireless network you are trying to connect to? Many notebooks come equipped with a special manufacturer's configuration utility, such as Toshiba's ConfigFree, in addition to standard OS connectivity software, like the "View Available Wireless Networks" option in modern Windows versions. In addition, there should be a little wireless icon in the system tray, which flashes a small bubble announcement when it connects or fails to connect. Floating the mouse pointer over the wireless icon in the system tray on a Windows desktop should show the name of the wireless connection (often a HEX address that looks like alphabet soup if not changed from the default), the speed (54 Mbps for 802.11G), the signal strength, and whether a connection to a router has been established. Note that a connection to a router does not imply a connection to the internet.

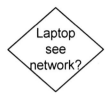

Manufacturer provided software can provide a much clearer picture of relative router distances and signal strength. In some circumstances, especially public networks at hotels, campuses and coffee shops, your laptop may consistently choose to connect to a weak router or access point when stronger signals are available. The manufacturer software usually does a better job identifying this problem than the five green signal strength bars of "View Available Wireless Networks."

Switch on, enabled? When a laptop doesn't see a wireless network, it's often because the wireless adapter is switched off or disabled in software. As with volume controls for laptop speakers, wireless networking can be disabled both manually and through software, and in more than one place. Most modern laptops come equipped with a manual switch on the front or side of the laptop that turns the wireless adapter on or off. There is usually an LED associated with the switch that will light only when the laptop's wireless capability is enabled. However, the LED may remain lit even if the wireless has been disabled in software, if it is a status indicator for the hardware switch only. The switch can easily be turned off by accident when picking up the laptop or when a book or other table clutter comes into contact with the side of the notebook, so it's a very common problem.

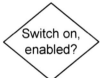

The easiest place in Windows to tell if the laptop wireless adapter has been disabled through software is in Device

Manager. One sure sign the adapter is disabled in software (or not operating properly) is if it doesn't appear in the system tray. If your laptop wireless adapter is discrete, a USB or PC card (PCMCIA) plug-in, shut down, make sure it's plugged in firmly, and reboot. Even if the wireless device is designed to be hot-swappable (plugged in while the laptop is turned on) it's better to shut down and do it, since this will give the operating system a chance to reset.

Router active, in range? If there isn't a wireless network in range, the notebook certainly can't connect to it. It doesn't matter if your laptop once connected to a network at the spot you are trying to connect from today, the question is whether or not there's an active signal your laptop should be picking up now. The most obvious reason for the wireless router to be invisible to your laptop is if the router is turned off or out of range. Next comes the wireless function of the router being disabled, or the antenna being damaged or missing. If the router is in another room, something as simple as a door which is usually open and is now closed can make enough difference in signal strength to prevent a connection. The best way to start troubleshooting wireless problems is to take your laptop and plunk it down right next to the router you are trying to connect to. If the wireless activity LED on the router isn't on and active, either wireless has been disabled on the router or the router is faulty.

Home network? Wireless networks in the home often use the exact same equipment as those in Internet cafes and small businesses, but corporate and campus networks use more sophisticated routers. One of the features some network administrators of large businesses take advantage of is to hide their network from casual encounters with the outside world simply by instructing the routers not to announce their presence with an "I'm here" beacon. This is one step beyond enabling security, which would normally be done as well. If the router beacon is turned off, you'll need to get the exact network setting from the network admin or another computer on the network in order to set up the wireless connection.

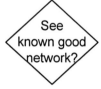

See known good network? This is the easiest, if not always the most convenient troubleshooting step. If you take the laptop to your neighbor's house or to the local cafe with free internet access, does the laptop at least see the existence of a known good network through either the OS view or the manufacturer's add-on software? If the laptop can't see a known good network with the wireless adapter turned on and enabled, the problem is with the laptop and not with your home router. Try disabling and enabling the wireless adapter, going through a full OS restart after each change. Try reinstalling the driver for the wireless adapter, and check the Internet for the most recent version of the driver available. The wireless adapter may have failed, but it's more likely a software problem. Don't rush into downloading the latest BIOS update for the notebook, especially if the wireless adapter is built-in, since it should work with the original BIOS and operating system.

Works security off? The inability to connect to a secured wireless network is usually due to the security working properly, as opposed to the way you thought it would work. If the first time you go to connect, the dialog box gets hung up on "Acquiring Network Address" you probably got the encryption key wrong. The first troubleshooting step for failure to connect to a secured wireless network in the home should always be turning off security on the router, rebooting, and seeing if the connection now works. There are several different levels of security available on most wireless routers, some of which aren't really thought of as security because they don't include encryption, such as MAC (Media Access Control) addressing. MAC filters allow you to establish a sort of a white list for network connections. The router won't make a connection to any wireless device that doesn't know it's MAC address (usually included on the router label). But in the absence of any other security, MAC filters will allow any laptop that has the MAC address typed in to connect without further ado.

WPA (Wi-Fi Protected Access) uses real encryption to encrypt data on the wireless network, making it harder for outsiders to decode network traffic without the key, often listed as the WEP (Wired Equivalent Privacy) key. WPA is an improved version of WEP and has replaced it, but the terms are sometimes used interchangeably, especially when talking about the key. A lot of confusion arises from the length of the WEP key and the MAC addresses which are often typed improperly on the laptop the first time around. It's also possible to create an unique encryption key for the router, which the router uses to create keys for your computers. If your laptop is older than 2004, there's a good chance it won't support WPA unless the network adapter firmware can be updated. Your options are to run without any security on your router, run WEP, or purchase a new plug-in wireless adapter for your laptop (USB or PC Card) that supports WPA.

Works on Ethernet port? Can the laptop access the Internet if you connect it directly to the router with an Ethernet cable? This is normally a yellow 100BaseT cable with RJ-45 connectors provided with the router. If you have trouble wirelessly accessing the router to create or change settings, plugging directly in through an Ethernet port or USB (if so equipped) is recommended. The router may come with setup software, but it's also common to access the onboard setup software directly through your browser, which doesn't require a live Internet connection. You just type the IP address of your router into the address bar, and provide the default password, assuming you haven't changed it. Some standard IP addresses are 192.168.1.1 or 192.168.0.1, but it should be easy to Google up the info for your exact router model.

Firewall, security blocked? One good reason for a laptop to refuse to see the Internet, even when it's plugged directly into the router, is that the security settings on the laptop prevent it from making contact. The variations on what can go wrong here are far too in depth for a hardware troubleshooting flowchart, the best test is to disable the firewall software, reboot and try to connect. Unfortunately, disabling security software, including firewalls, isn't always easy to do, and may require talking to tech support at the security software company. If this is a laptop that belongs to your employer and has been set up to run on a corporate network, you should talk to your network administrator before taking any radical steps that may make it work at home but prevent it from connecting to the network at work.

Live Internet at router? It's not unusual for new DSL subscribers to try to set up their network as soon as the kit arrives from the phone company, before the phone company has enabled the line for DSL. It won't work. There's just no way your laptop can connect to the Internet through your router, wireless or not, if there's no DSL connection between the router and the phone company. Most routers come equipped with a status light for the Internet connection. If you cycle the power on the router (if there's no switch, you can pull the plug) you should see activity on the Internet LED as the router negotiates for and gains an Internet connection. It may take five minutes or longer for a modem to negotiate a new connection under certain conditions, so don't give up too quickly. If the modem can't negotiate a connection after being powered up, it should display an error state. The modem LED reporting a live Internet connection doesn't absolutely guarantee that the connection is good or that the router is functioning properly, but the problem is much more likely to be on the laptop end.

If the LED doesn't show an Internet connection, get on the phone with the ISP, usually the telco or cable company. The fault could be with the ISP, it could be with the router, or it could be with the land lines. While a land line problem is the responsibility of the ISP if it's outside your house, it doesn't hurt to walk outside and see if there's an obvious tree branch lying on the line or something, just so you'll know for sure what the problem is. In the case of DSL, if the telephone still works, the line should be OK, as long as you didn't damage the line to the modem or unplug it from the wall. With a cable modem, if the TV works, the cable connection to the house is good, and any cabling problem would be with the line to the modem. If you're a new DSL customer and you live too far from the telephone company switching gear, it's possible that DSL won't work in your location, even though they delivered the equipment and turned on the service.

Default settings on router? Don't trust your memory, restore the router settings to default through the router console accessed by the IP address or accompanying software. Unplugging the router does not reset the defaults, which are stored in non volatile memory. If restoring the router defaults, cycling the power and rebooting the laptop doesn't allow you to connect, just go back one step and continue, answering "Yes" to default settings at the router.

Intermittent connection? The most frustrating problems to troubleshoot on wireless networks are intermittent connections. Logic seems to dictate that if it works sometimes, it should work all the time, but mismatched hardware or protocols can result in intermittent operation, as can interference, failing hardware, or a poor signal from the ISP. However, the most common reason for intermittent connections is a weak signal that appears to be stronger than it actually is on the reported signal strength.

Probably the best indicator of a marginal wireless signal is slow operation, but if your notebook came equipped with a utility that truly shows the relative strength of signals and your connection is usually on the borderline, a weak signal is likely the problem. Relocate the laptop closer to the router or move the router to a more central location in the workspace.

Same ver. (b/g/n) 802.11? The IEEE standard for wireless Ethernet networks using 802.11 versions b,g,n and y are supposed to be backwards compatible, but in practice, not all of the hardware produced lives up to the standard. In fact, when you get into using repeaters, it's best to keep to one family or brand of products for all of your wireless broadcast equipment. Most newer notebooks have 802.11 b/g/n wireless capability built-in and they will normally work with older routers, but older notebooks and PC adapter cards of the 802.11b generation often have trouble with 802.11g routers. Some routers default to the pure 802.11g or 802.11n mode unless you specifically choose the backward compatibility modes, and doing so may degrade performance for all users.

Laptop works public network? Once you've done all the troubleshooting you can at home and possibly at a friendly neighbor's as well, the last test is to drag the laptop out to a cafe or other location where a wireless network is offered as a draw to customers. If your laptop does connect on the public network, it indicates that the problem is either with your router hardware, your ISP, or the router settings. Even though you've restored the default router settings by this point, make absolutely sure wireless is enabled and security is disabled.

If your laptop won't connect to the public network, it's entirely possible that your wireless adapter is at fault, you can try a USB or PC card wireless adapter if you're willing to have it sticking out of the side of the notebook. But most of the time the problem will be software. Either the wireless adapter is, in fact, disabled in some way you haven't been able to spot, the driver version isn't the best for the adapter model (even if Device Manager appears happy), or there's some corruption in the networking settings that you can't figure out. If you search the web, there are some free third party utilities you can run to fix the registry, the network stack and network settings by resetting them to defaults, and which report out on the process if they find errors.

Phone, Bluetooth interfere? If your wireless connection slows down or gets flaky when you or somebody else in the household is using a cellular phone, Bluetooth device or other RF emitter, the problem is interference. There is no cure other than trying to increase the distance between the laptop and the interfering device or not using the interfering device when you're on the Internet. However, interference is a much less common problem than flaky hardware, an intermittent signal from the ISP due to land-line or weather conditions (rain degrading signals or wind knocking the cables around on the poles) or software timeouts. Overheating hardware can lead to intermittent operation, as can loose connections and power interruptions. Keep in mind that a properly functioning laptop has its own built-in UPS (Uninterruptible Power Source) in the form of the main battery that should provide seamless operation so you might not even notice if your power grid is suffering from brownouts or even mini-blackouts. The router, however, may be resetting every time the power glitches, and then requiring a few minutes to reestablish the Internet connection each time.

Motherboard, CPU, RAM Failure

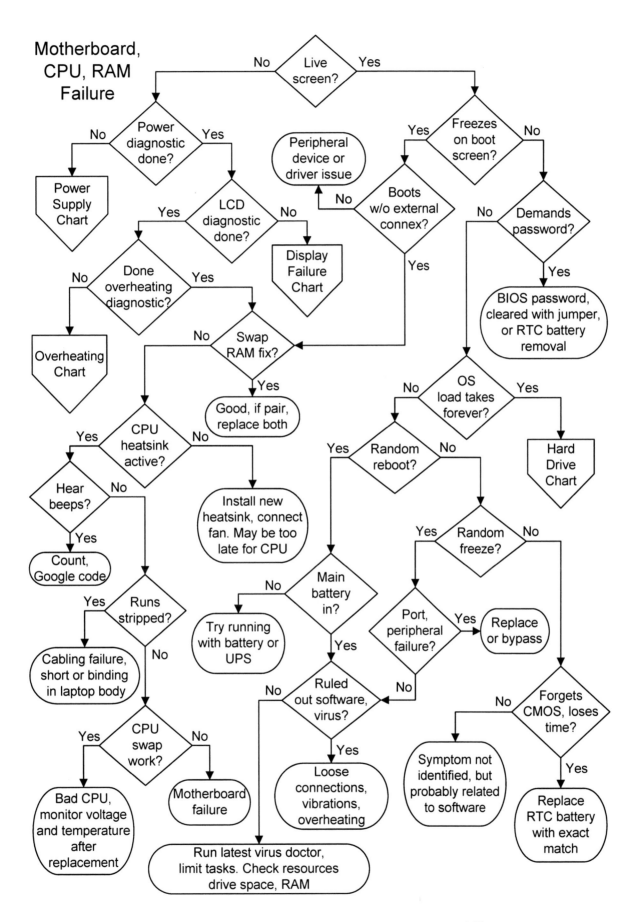

Live screen? Does the screen show any signs that the laptop is alive and thinking? If it does, the motherboard hasn't failed outright, though it may turn out to suffer from partial failure or intermittent problems. If you get nothing on the LCD but the system works fine if you connect it to an external monitor, you should skip to video diagnostics from this point.

Power diagnostic done? Do you see any LEDs flashing, hear any beeps, drives spinning up, fans, etc. Laptops are all equipped with status LEDs, normally including an LED for power on, an LED showing the AC Adapter is attached and functioning, and an LED to show the battery is present and charging. If the power isn't coming on, proceed to power failure diagnostics. If the power diagnostics sends you back here, continue following through the diagnostic steps.

LCD diagnostic done? If you haven't performed the video failure diagnostics for a dead screen yet, do so now. Remember that in the vast majority of laptop computers, the video processor shares the same physical memory modules with the CPU. If the diagnostic points to a video processor failure, make sure to search the Internet to see if it's a characteristic failure for that model with a possible workaround, like reflowing the solder.

Done overheating diagnostic? This is particularly important in the case of dead screen troubleshooting if the problem only occurs when the laptop is warmed up. All of the components in your laptop are subject to failure if the laptop gets too hot, including vital motherboard components, the CPU and the RAM. If your laptop is overheating and you ignore the fact, you might properly diagnose the component that is failing when it gets too hot and replace it, but unless that component was itself responsible for the overheating, you've treated the symptom without finding the cure.

Swap RAM fix? Many technicians will start troubleshooting any dead screen or no boot failure by swapping out the memory, because it's easily done and it's often at fault. If you have two RAM modules installed you can try running one and then the other, and if you can borrow a compatible module from a friend, it will rarely damage their RAM to try it in your system. While we hate to recommend you go out and purchase a part just to try it out, a replacement memory module for your system may run as little as $20. If your existing RAM turns out to be good and the problem is solved later on, you'll be able to install the spare, increasing your capacity and performance. For most home users who have never taken a laptop apart before, swapping the RAM is a good gamble before we get to taking the laptop completely apart.

CPU heatsink active? All modern laptop CPUs require a heatsink, and most of these are an active heatsink, with a fan on top, or a hood over the CPU heatsink with a fan blowing air through. Laptops offer heat and power management at both the operating system and BIOS level. You may be able to set the exact temperature in CMOS Setup for which you want the fan to come on or the system to warn of thermal overload and shut down. In the operating system, you can generally tweak the CPU settings so it consumes less power (resulting in lower performance and less heat) or for quiet operation, which limits fan usage.

If you just installed a replacement CPU and powered the system up with no heatsink as a test, you may have damaged the new CPU already. If the fan on your active heatsink isn't spinning up, replace the fan and hope for the best. Make sure to confirm the new heatsink fan is operating after replacement since it could be the power point on the motherboard that's failed. You should never need to replace the heatsink itself unless you break the hold-down mechanism, since it's just a chunk of metal. If you replace the entire active heatsink, make sure that it's designed for your specific model, or it may fail to contact the CPU even with the proper application of thermal paste, guaranteeing failure.

Hear beeps? If you have a system that powers up, the next question is, do you hear any beeps coming from the laptop. If your motherboard doesn't have a dedicated piezoelectric speaker for beep codes, it will use the built-in laptop speakers. The beeps should come in repeated patterns, so many in a row, and then repeated. Write down what you hear and then head to Google and search for the translation of the code. If you hear an unending string of beeps, it's often bad RAM if the screen is dead, or a keyboard failure if the screen is live. Depending on the manufacturer, you might also get specific beep codes for CPU failure or video processor failure. Many beep codes have been abandoned since they pertained to non-user replaceable surface mount components. It never hurts to shut down and reseat the system RAM if you're getting a beep code.

Runs stripped? Bench testing laptop motherboards is quite different from bench testing PC motherboards because laptops are engineered as a unit and it's not easy to run the motherboard out of the case. The option is to simply strip everything not essential for a live screen out of the laptop to ensure that there isn't a problem with a component that is putting an undue mechanical stress or electrical load on the motherboard. The RAM and the CPU need to remain installed, but you can remove the hard drive and the DVD drive, and if you're ambitious to take the whole laptop apart, you can try for a live screen without the keyboard or any non-essential daughter cards installed. You should always unplug the AC adapter and remove the battery while working on the laptop, but you'll have to plug the AC adapter back in again to attempt to boot.

CPU swap works? If you still have a "no signs of life" situation with the motherboard powered up and stripped down, it's either a motherboard component failure or the CPU. Swap in a known good CPU if you can get one dirt cheap or free, not forgetting to install a good heatsink and to connect the fan, even just for a quick test. You need to find a CPU that's supported by the laptop BIOS, it's not enough to find one that mechanically fits the socket, assuming the CPU isn't soldered into place! The only way to determine what CPUs are appropriate is to check your user manual or do a little research on the web. Think twice and three times about the value of your laptop before spending real money on a new CPU, since you're just gambling the problem isn't a motherboard failure. If your old CPU is bad and the heatsink fan is dead, it's a pretty sure bet that the dead fan caused the CPU to failure.

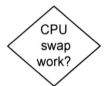

You can identify many motherboard component failures with a decent magnifying glass. They'll show burnt or melted spots, discoloration, or be carbonized right out of existence. Some discrete motherboard components such as capacitors and power semiconductors are replaceable with a good soldering iron, though there's always a chance they'll pop again as soon as you power up if the fault lay higher upstream. Other surface mount components are barely visible to the eye, require an insider's access to replacement parts, and expensive soldering equipment to attempt to install.

There's no point in calling the manufacturer to price a new motherboard if you determine it's the most likely problem. Laptop motherboards are specific to the model and family, and the manufacturers charge you almost as much as a brand new laptop for most replacement motherboards. If the laptop is relatively new or beloved and you really want to keep it going, the best option is to try to find a replacement motherboard on eBay from a pull, from another failed laptop with a different problem like a bad LCD. There's always the risk the replacement will be bad as well, but in shopping, you may find that a second hand working laptop of your exact model is available for less than you would have thought. You can buy it and move your hard drive over in a jiffy, but make sure you don't end up paying as much as the price of a new, superior notebook.

Freezes on boot screen? Does the system power right up, give a happy beep or two, then freeze on the BIOS screen? First try removing any external connections, including your networking, cellular modem or dial-up modem cord, printer cables, anything that wasn't attached to the laptop when you took it out of the box for the first time. If this allows the laptop to boot, the problem is either with one of the peripherals you disconnected (check by process of elimination) or with the software driver for that peripheral. Windows based systems may automatically start in Safe Mode after being powered down and rebooted if the problem was with a driver.

Demands password? Does your system power right up and demand a password? We're talking about pre-OS load here (a BIOS screen password), not a Windows password. This normally pops up in a small text box in the dead center of the screen, which may be dark but for the box. Some newer laptops are equipped with fingerprint scanners or other biometric locks, but these give you the option to type in a password as a fallback. If you know that a password is set but you've forgotten it, you may be in for a headache. It's also possible that somebody in your family ended up entering CMOS Setup and set the password by accident. Unfortunately, if the machine is asking for a password on boot, it may also demand a password to access CMOS Setup in order to disable it.

Check with the manufacturer's tech support and do a Google search to see if there's a workaround before taking the laptop apart. Desktop motherboards come equipped with the equivalent of a "Forget Password" jumper, but laptops usually aren't that friendly. There's a good chance that the password is cleared by removing the RTC (Real Time Clock) battery that also preserves the CMOS settings. You should search the web for instructions for your model, as it may involve a whole complex sequence of events, like removing the RTC battery, AC adapter and main battery and then holding in the power switch.

OS load takes forever? Does the OS load take forever or does the system get as far as complaining about a missing boot drive, a bad disk, missing operating system, no boot partition, anything similar? If you get any of these messages, proceed to hard drive failure diagnostics. If the system doesn't freeze on the BIOS screen, but doesn't start loading the OS either, it could be a rapid overheating problem with a critical motherboard component, but the odds are still with software. One check is to change the boot order in CMOS to boot the DVD/CD drive first, and to try a bootable disc. If the disc boots and the laptop sits quietly without freezing up, the problem is with the hard drive or installed software.

Random reboot? Does the system reboot itself for no apparent reason, either during the boot process or at any point once you're up and running? Random reboots are often caused by mechanical or thermal problems. Mechanical problems include little bits of conductor flopping around inside the laptop, vibrations caused by airplanes, tapping your foot on the floor or typing on the keyboard! Remember that the whole laptop is crammed into this narrow little box and the connectors are fairly fragile. You can eliminate flaky mechanical issues by trying a USB keyboard and mouse and not touching the laptop while operating. If that solves the problem, you know the reboots are due to vibration. For thermal problems, see the overheating flowchart.

A random reboot is sometimes caused by a Windows operating system setting. This can be solved by going to System Properties and selecting the Advanced tab, then the Settings tab under Startup and Recovery. Clear the checkmark under System Failure – Automatically Restart. It might solve the problem, or it might lead to a BSOD (Blue Screen of Death) error that helps diagnose the underlying cause, often RAM.

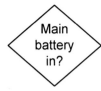

Main battery installed? If not, try running with the battery installed, or try running your AC adapter though a UPS (Uninterruptable Power Supply). The problem may be with your electrical power grid, either brown-outs, surges, or poor regulation. Testing with the battery installed makes more sense than running out and buying a UPS, unless you have one available, but some laptop owners see extending battery life by storing it in ideal conditions when not traveling as half the fun of ownership.

Ruled out software, virus? If you don't have an up-to-date malware protection suite installed, including anti-virus, anti-spyware, and anti-adware and a firewall, you haven't even begun to eliminate invasive software as the root of your problem. Installing all of this protective software after the fact will usually make you aware of a malware problem, but it may be too late to cure it without extensive Google research on your part. The "good" software is designed to keep the "bad" software out. Getting rid of "bad software" once it's established on your laptop is more dicey.

Software lock-ups can also occur because of data corruption or operating system registry confusion. While reinstalling the operating system and starting over from scratch is the dodge of somebody who can't pinpoint the problem, it's often the only practical solution for the casual laptop user. You should run the standard operating system clean-up chores before giving up. Windows offers a number of hard drive maintenance tasks under System Tools.

Random freeze? Is your laptop suffering from random lockups? We're talking about lockups that you need to power off and on to clear. If you can CRTL-ALT-DEL your way out of a lock-up, in fact, if you can get any response with it at all, it's more likely a software conflict or incompatibility. Although the CPU, RAM and motherboard are all candidates for intermittent lock-ups, the hard drive and motherboard connections are also possible. Overheating is always suspect in random lockups.

If you call tech support with these symptoms, they may recommend that you flash the BIOS to the latest version. The procedure is simple, you download the software from the manufacturer's website and the process is automatic when you run the program, but BEWARE. If you grab the wrong version of the BIOS off the web, if the manufacturer has made a mistake, if you can't quite determine which revision of a motherboard you have, or if the process gets interrupted in the middle by a power spike, etc, you can lose the motherboard. In other words, if the BIOS doesn't get completely installed or isn't correct, you can never boot the system again to fix it. But if you've concluded that the only option is buying a new motherboard or a new laptop, it's worth a try.

If the problem is with an external peripheral, the first step is to inspect and reseat the cable connecting the device to the laptop. If it's a USB peripheral, the best test of both the device and the cable is to connect to another computer and see if it works. If it does, the problem is with the port hardware or the driver (see the keyboard, mouse and USB troubleshooting flowchart). If the port is physically loose or damaged, the repair requires resoldering or replacing on the motherboard. Try a different USB port on the laptop and try reinstalling any driver software for the device.

Forgets CMOS, loses time? If your laptop keeps forgetting the time and the date, or gives you an error message about CMOS settings every time you power on, your RTC (Real Time Clock) battery has probably died. This battery is entirely distinct from the main battery that powers your laptop or the auxiliary battery some laptops featured for preserving memory in suspend states. It's a little battery mounted on the motherboard, usually a small disk like a wrist watch battery, and while they are widely available and inexpensive, gaining access to the motherboard to do the job can be a nightmare in some laptops. If you don't have a user's manual with step by step instructions, search the web for a photograph illustrated guide for your exact model family.

Boots w/o external connex? If the laptop boots up fine when you power up without any external connections, the problem is with the external device or with the software driver for it. External connections here include anything that isn't part of the basic laptop, including: docking stations, port replicators, security devices, PC cards, USB devices, telephone and networking cables, an external video connection, speakers or a microphone. Don't start trying to analyze why the device can't affect boot in your case, just try without it.

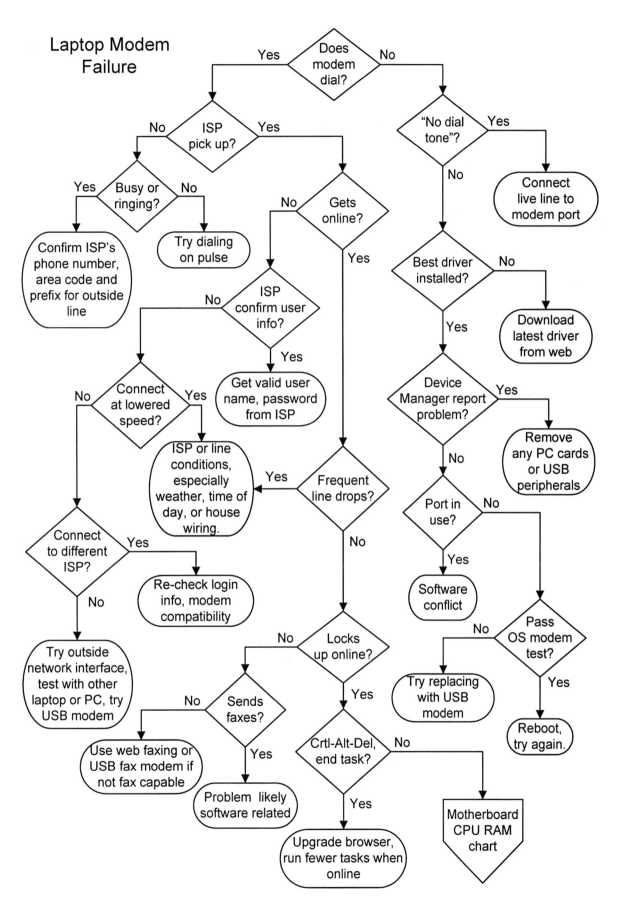

Laptop Modem Failure

151

Does modem dial? The first question for a dial-up modem is, does your modem actually dial the phone? Some laptops feature a little piezoelectric speaker on a modem/network daughter card, but others use the laptop speakers as a modem annunciator. Many people (and computer vendors) turn down the volume for this in software, which on Windows machines is buried somewhere in the modem properties reached through Control Panel. For laptop computers that run the sound through the speakers, the volume controls in Windows and any exterior volume controls must be turned up. If you can't hear Windows chimes, music CD's, or downloaded audio through your speakers, odds are you won't hear the modem dialing either.

ISP pick up? You should be able to hear the ISP's modem pick up and whistle and hiss back at your modem through the speaker. If not, make sure you are dialing the right phone number and that the ISP isn't temporarily down. Just dial the number from a regular phone handset and the ISP modem should pick up and whistle or hiss at you. Make sure you have the area code and any prefix for an outside line correct, especially if you are dialing from a business. Dial-up lines in a business must have a clean path through a business phone system (PBX - Private Branch eXchange), just like fax lines. Dialing "9" for an outside line is quite common in small business settings. If the phone is always busy, call the ISP's tech support or try one of the other phone numbers they provide. It could simply be that they don't have enough modems available for the traffic in your area at certain times of day.

Busy or ringing? If you hear the modem dial but the dial tone remains steady until an operator recording picks up and tells you that your phone is off hook, you're trying to use "tone" dialing on a "pulse" system. This is easily changed in the "Dialing Properties" of the basic modem page in Control Panel of Windows systems. If a stranger picks up the phone and yells at you, you've dialed the wrong number.

Gets online? If you get an error stating that the ISP can't negotiate a connection, protocol, or anything along those lines, you definitely aren't getting online. Unfortunately, this error is too generic to help much with troubleshooting. Even messages telling you to check your password can be caused by just about anything. Try redialing several times without changing anything

to make sure you aren't just encountering an overloaded modem pool.

ISP confirm user info? Call your ISP on the phone to confirm your login information if it's the first time you're dialing in. Re-enter your password, remembering that caps usually count. Assuming you have your username and password right, the odds are any errors reported aren't due to any protocol settings on your part, especially if you haven't changed the defaults. If the error crops up at random, it's usually due to the weather and the time of day, as both play a major role in the circuit conditions of the telco infrastructure. Stormy or damp weather can badly degrade the lines of older telephone networks. The time of day is also important, with the beginning of the business day, and a period in the mid-afternoon usually being the worst times.

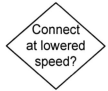

Connect at lower speed? Does your modem connect at a speed in the 20 Kb/s to 40 Kb/s range? The connection speed is usually announced on screen before the connection window disappears, and can be checked at any time through the connection icon in the system tray. There are several possibilities, but the most likely is that your modem is capable of a much higher connection speed than the circuit, for various reasons, can support. A long delay in getting online is due to endless negotiation between your modem and the ISP modem as they slowly ratchet down the speed on both ends until a satisfactory error rate is reached. This could be due to a failing modem, but it's more often infrastructure or line conditions that limit connection speed.

Your connection speed will always be lower than the 56 Kb/s modem rating in the U.S. because it's limited to 53 Kb/s by law. Laptops with 56 Kb/s modems should get connections ranging from 48 Kb/s to 53 Kb/s in ideal conditions. If your speed is always lower, it could be that your modem speed is actually set too low in software, or that you are using some error checking or compression algorithm that isn't ideal for the circuit. Make a note of all of your current settings before you start making changes, and note that in some cases, you'll have to reboot before they take effect. Make sure you check the Extra Settings field in the modem connection Advanced Properties menu in Windows. It could also be that your phone wiring simply isn't going to support a higher speed, that you are too far from the central office, or they just haven't upgraded their infrastructure to support digital signaling, in which case you'll never get a connection over 33K. If you're traveling away from your usual modem pool, it could be that the local ISP doesn't fully support higher speeds.

Connect to different ISP? The best test for eliminating modem failure is to see if it will connect to a different service. If you can connect to a friend's ISP or a free bulletin board, it's a definite proof that the modem isn't bad. If you can't connect to another ISP, it doesn't prove your modem is faulty, it could still be a problem with line conditions, standards or logins. But if you can use another laptop or PC to connect over the same line to the ISP, the problem is clearly in your laptop.

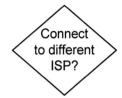

No dial tone? If the software reports, "No dial tone", you have to test if the phone line is live or if an off-hook phone elsewhere on the circuit has caused the line to drop. Check the phone jack at the wall with a telephone handset. If the wall jack is good, try changing the telephone patch cord running from your laptop modem port to the jack. If the wall jack is dead and the other phones on the circuit work, you need to repair the in-wall wiring or use a different jack.

Best driver installed? Have you installed the most recent modem driver you can find on the laptop manufacturer's web site? Even if your laptop is brand-new, they sometimes ship with obsolete drivers, either because your model is a close-out that has been sitting on the shelf somewhere for a year, or because problems with the driver software have been discovered since your unit was manufactured.

 Device Manager report problem? The status of the modem hardware and driver as understood by the operating system appears in Device Manager in Windows. There's not much likelihood of a conflict with another device in a laptop since they are engineered to work together, but it's a good idea to try unplugging all external devices while troubleshooting. Try finding an updated driver on the manufacturer's website and installing. Try the interactive troubleshooting wizard in Device Manager. If you can't resolve the Device Manager problem, either the modem is bad or the daughter card (if your model features a separate card for the modem and networking) has come loose in its connector. Check your owner's manual or the web to see if the latter is a possibility, and if so, find exact

illustrated disassembly instructions for your model before you attempt to check. Before trying, identify what other components are on the daughter card (like a 100BaseT network connection), and if they still function, it's unlikely that reseating the daughter card will help.

Port in use? Does the operating system or dialing software report the port is "in use" when you try to dial? Try shutting down and rebooting. The "port in use" error is due to another active software application claiming the port the modem is set on. You could get this error if you're already using the modem but don't realize it for some reason, but it's more likely that you've recently installed obsolete software for synchronizing an old palm device or a camera that's colliding with the modem driver.

Pass OS modem test? In Windows Control Panel > Modems and Phones, find the "Diagnostics" tab (exact location varies between Windows versions) select your modem, and look for an option like "Query Modem" or "More Info." If Windows can't talk to the modem and get a response, without the modem being hooked up to anything, the modem hardware is bad or the daughter board carrying the modem is loose.

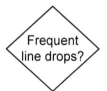

Frequent line drops? Do you suffer from frequent disconnects? The first thing to check if you have line drops is whether you have call waiting and a modem/ISP that doesn't support call waiting. If you don't have call waiting, line drops are usually a result of the ISP being over burdened, or really bad line conditions. The ISP will rarely admit that their system is dropping lines, so it's a tough one to diagnose with 100% certainty. There's nothing you can do about the telco infrastructure, but you can get the cleanest connection possible in your house by reducing the number of connections between your laptop and the incoming phone line. You can also try running your modem at a lower speed. You may determine that the problem is with the infrastructure of the telephone company or some other external factors, such as the wiring in your part of town being routed alongside an incredibly noisy electrical transformer, etc. There's nothing you can do about the weather, but you can work around the time of day problem by identifying the good times to call in and sticking with them.

The Laptop Repair Workbook

Locks up online? Does the whole computer sometimes lock-up when you're online, forcing you to shut down and reboot? If it always happens at the same web site, then it's probably an incompatibility with the web browser version and software plug-ins. You may need to enable Java Script or download and install a browser upgrade to access certain sites. The important point is, if the lock-up only occurs on certain sites, it's not a modem issue.

Ctrl-Alt-Del end task? If you can get a live task list with Ctrl- Alt-Del, shut down the browser and continue, it's probably a software conflict or an incompatible web application. Browsers sometimes lock-up if you try to access your favorites list before the browser has finished loading. You could also be suffering lock-ups due to RAM or CPU overheating problems, so take a look through the Motherboard, CPU and RAM Failure diagnostics.

Sends Faxes? Do you want to send or receive faxes but you can't figure out how? The first thing to check is whether or not you have a Fax/Modem. If it wasn't sold as a fax/modem and the driver doesn't identify it as a fax modem, it's not a fax and you can't directly use it to send and receive faxes. You can still use a web based fax service or buy a USB fax/modem. If your laptop does include a fax/modem and can't fax, it's just a question of installing (or finding) the proper software, which should have come on CD with the fax/modem.

DVD/CD Playback and Record

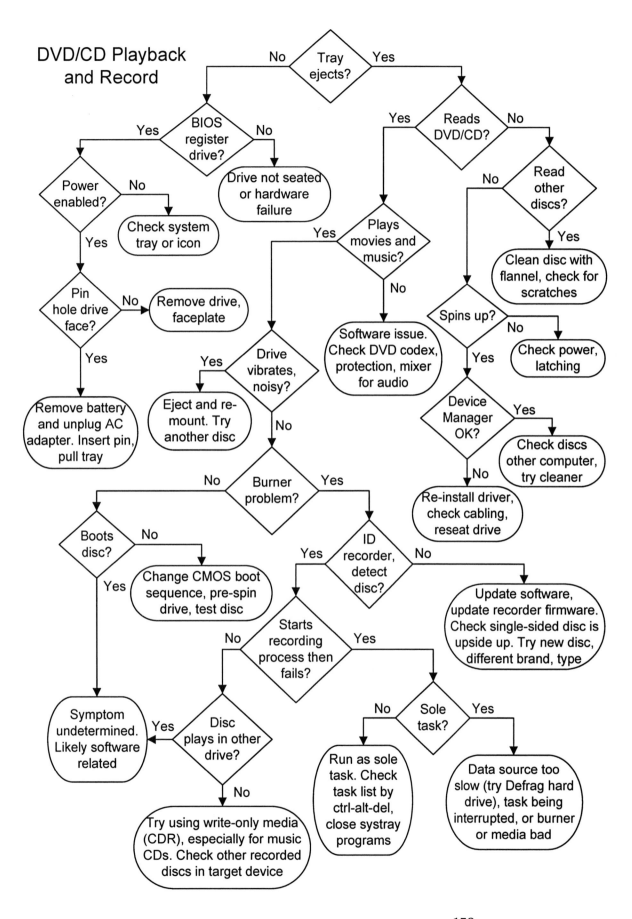

Tray ejects?
- No → **BIOS register drive?**
  - Yes → **Power enabled?**
    - No → Check system tray or icon
    - Yes → **Pin hole drive face?**
      - No → Remove drive, faceplate
      - Yes → Remove battery and unplug AC adapter. Insert pin, pull tray
  - No → Drive not seated or hardware failure
- Yes → **Reads DVD/CD?**
  - Yes → **Plays movies and music?**
    - Yes → **Drive vibrates, noisy?**
      - Yes → Eject and re-mount. Try another disc
      - No → **Burner problem?**
        - No → **Boots disc?**
          - No → Change CMOS boot sequence, pre-spin drive, test disc
          - Yes → Symptom undetermined. Likely software related
        - Yes → **ID recorder, detect disc?**
          - Yes → **Starts recording process then fails?**
            - No → **Disc plays in other drive?**
              - Yes → Symptom undetermined. Likely software related
              - No → Try using write-only media (CDR), especially for music CDs. Check other recorded discs in target device
            - Yes → **Sole task?**
              - No → Run as sole task. Check task list by ctrl-alt-del, close systray programs
              - Yes → Data source too slow (try Defrag hard drive), task being interrupted, or burner or media bad
          - No → Update software, update recorder firmware. Check single-sided disc is upside up. Try new disc, different brand, type
    - No → Software issue. Check DVD codex, protection, mixer for audio
  - No → **Read other discs?**
    - Yes → Clean disc with flannel, check for scratches
    - No → **Spins up?**
      - No → Check power, latching
      - Yes → **Device Manager OK?**
        - Yes → Check discs other computer, try cleaner
        - No → Re-install driver, check cabling, reseat drive

Tray ejects? The most basic and potentially most disastrous problem that can occur with a CD or DVD drive is a stuck tray. Will the tray eject when you press the eject button? Press it once, like a doorbell, and then move your finger away, or you may be sending it repeated open and close commands. The drive won't pop right open if it is actively playing a disc. If you're trying to eject a disc using software (clicking on a software eject button on the screen) and it doesn't work, try the manual button on the drive.

BIOS register drive? If the tray still doesn't eject, reboot again and note whether the BIOS registers the drive. Some laptops don't report installed hardware on a boot screen, so you'll have to access CMOS Setup to check. If the BIOS doesn't register the drive, it's dropped dead or there's a problem with the controller (motherboard) or the connection in the bay. Reseating the drive in the bay is the next step, easy if it's a swappable bay, a little harder if it's held in with a screw from the bottom of the laptop.

Power Enabled? If the drive is registered by the BIOS and doesn't show any errors in Device Manager, you really may have a stuck tray. But the first step is to determine if the drive has been locked in software and the eject button has been disabled. Laptops often give the user the option to disable power to the optical drive in order to save a little battery juice or to prevent the tray from ejecting when you least expect it. Disabling the optical drive power really isn't a bad policy if you rarely use it, as it helps to protect the tray, which is fragile when it extends from the drive. Another test is to see if the eject button works immediately after powering up the laptop, before the operating system has a chance to load.

Pin hole drive face? The next step is to look for a pinhole on the front of the DVD/CD drive. Power down the laptop, unplug the power cord and remove the battery. Straighten out a couple inches worth of paper clip, the heaviest gauge that will fit in the hole. Gently push the paper clip straight into the hole, until you feel it depress the release mechanism. This will sometime cause the tray to pop out a fraction of an inch, other times you will have to pry it a little to get it started. Once you have enough tray sticking out to grab it with your fingers, you should be able to pull it out, though it can offer quite a bit of resistance, and you may damage whatever disc is inside. If the faceplate seems to be bulging as you pull, the disc is hung up on it, and the best thing to do is remove the drive from the laptop and then remove the faceplate.

The faceplate is normally held on by simple plastic clips working from the inside out, or attached with tiny screws. Depress clips into the side of the drive while removing the faceplate so you don't break them off. If you have removed the drive from the laptop, tried the manual pinhole release, removed the faceplate and still can't get the tray out, you have a problem. If there's a mechanical failure, it probably isn't repairable without access to special tools and parts. If the drive contains a valuable disc, you should be able to dismantle the drive to the point where you can rescue the disc without scratching it.

Reads DVD/CD? When you mount a disc, whether a movie, data, software or music, does the drive acknowledge that a disc is present and let you view the contents? It doesn't matter at this point of the troubleshooting process whether or not you can get through installing the software on the disc, play it properly, or read all of the information. The question is simply, can the drive see anything at all on the disc?

Read other discs? Try a stamped factory disc, as opposed to a recordable disc. If it works, the problem is with the media and not the drive. Clean the problem disc with a soft bit of flannel. The discs are plastics, so don't use solvents. Scratches can render a disc unreadable, including scratches on the label surface, which can cause distortions in the optical layer that is actually being read from the bottom. Try the disc in another reader before chucking it out, it could just have trouble with the drive in your laptop.

Spins up? As long as the power to the drive is good and it responds to the eject button, it should give any disc a preliminary spin as soon as it's installed so it can inform the operating system what's there. The drive should go through the motions of doing this even if the disc itself is faulty or there are problems with the drive in software. The LED on the drive or the LED on the laptop that shows DVD/CD drive activity (if so equipped) should be active when the drive spins up.

Device Manager OK? Does your laptop drive show up as operating properly in Windows Device Manager. Are there any little symbols next to it, like a red "X" or error messages shown with the drive? If so, the first step is to reinstall the driver. Download the latest driver from the manufacturer's website and install it. If you've upgraded to a new version of the operating system, or have allowed automated updates to the operating system over the Internet, your existing driver may turn out to be incompatible. If Device Manager only reports a problem with the hardware after the most recent driver is installed, you can try to remove it and reinstall the old driver. Check the Internet for a firmware upgrade for the drive, though it really shouldn't be necessary for basic compatibility. If that doesn't help and you don't have another laptop available to test if the drive still works, you might want to consider replacing it with an external USB drive rather than buying an exact replacement. The problem could turn out to be a broken connector or failed controller on the motherboard.

Plays movies and music? If a drive won't play a movie but can read DVD data discs, or won't play music but can read CD data discs, the problem is due to software. The media player you are using may display a specific error message, like telling you the screen properties must be set to a certain resolution and number of colors for a movie to play. Or, the player may report that it can't find a decoder (CODEC) to play the particular disc. Even if the movie worked last night, your media player may have received an automated update the next time you went online that rendered the installed CODEC obsolete. If you search the Internet, you'll find plenty of people trying to sell you CODECs, but if you use Google and stay away from the advertisements, you should be able to get the updated version for free.

You may also encounter new copy protection schemes that render some discs unplayable on your laptop, even though you aren't trying to copy them. The only solution for this again lays in software and Internet research for the specific failure. It may turn out that the only way to render your DVD player compatible with a new type of copy protection is to update the DVD drive firmware. If an update isn't available for your particular model, you can end up out of luck when it comes to playing certain discs from certain studios after a particular date.

Drive vibrates, noisy? Does the drive cause the whole laptop to tremble when it spins up? High speed drives will vibrate like crazy if a disc is off balance, either because it was chucked up wrong on the spindle, or because the disc itself has some weighting problem. Aside from obvious physical flaws (like the dog or the kid took a bite out of the edge of the disc) a misapplied label can create an unbalanced disc. Try ejecting and reinserting the disc, but don't keep running a disc in a drive if it vibrates badly. The disc could end up damaging the drive (discs have been known to shatter at high speeds) and it doesn't do the other components in your system any good to be vibrated, which can lead to connections working apart or worse. Your operating system may give you an option to run the drive at lower speed, usually in the interest of quieter operation. If the problem only occurs with some discs, you can blame the discs. Otherwise, consider an external USB drive replacement, and save the internal drive for emergency use while traveling.

Burner problem? Does your problem involve recording CDs or DVDs? Recording problems are largely independent of reading and playback problems. The drive uses a different wavelength laser and much higher power when recording, and the recording media is often at the heart of recording problems. We concentrate on problems that are caused by hardware or software failure going forward, but keep in mind if you're trying to copy discs that recording may fail due to various copy protection schemes.

Boots disc? Does your system refuse to boot known good boot discs, like operating systems or purpose made virus recovery discs? Don't assume a disc is good because it's supposed to be, try booting it in another system. Next try setting the boot sequence in CMOS Setup to boot to the CD or DVD first. This shouldn't really be necessary if the hard drive is brand new or has been wiped out, but can fix the problem if the installed operating system is corrupted. If you're using an external USB drive to boot a known good disc and CMOS Setup lets you select an external USB boot device but it still doesn't work, it may only work with a JumpDrive. Some high speed external drives take too long to spin up a disc, and fail to report to the BIOS that there's a bootable disc present before the BIOS gives up.

ID recorder, detect disc? Does the recording software installed on the laptop see the burner and correctly identify it? Get the latest version of the software from the third party web site. The fact that the software was packaged with your drive when you bought it doesn't necessarily mean it's up-to-date for your particular model or the operating system release you're running.

Some known incompatibilities exist with virus software, which will prompt you to download patches. You may find, through the website of your laptop manufacturer or through the website of the third party software vendor, that your DVD/CD recorder requires a firmware update to operate with some recent operating system or recording software release that you've been automatically updated to use.

Does the recorder software detect that a recordable disc is in the drive? The most common error when using cheap discs sold without any labeling is mounting them in the drive tray upside down. You can try turning it over, or if there are numbers printed around the spindle hole in the center of the disc, the disc is upside up when you can read them. Try cleaning the disc. It may be bad, even if it looks perfectly good to the eye with no scratches, fingerprints, etc. Failure rates can run as high as 20% or more with cheap discs that have been sitting around for a while on a spindle. Make sure the disc type you purchased is compatible with your recorder, even if it means trying a more expensive brand the manufacturer recommends.

Starts recording process then fails? Note that this renders the "write only" or "R" as in CDR or DVDR media useless. The first thing to check is if the drive successfully records discs to completion at a lower speed, starting with the lowest speed possible. If your recorder works at lower record speeds, the recordable media you have may not be certified for the higher speed, or it may just not work at the higher speed in your recorder. You may also be suffering from a buffer underrun, where the recorder runs out of data to write to the disc and fails. In today's era of even the slowest hardware being pretty fast, this is usually due to other tasks overtaxing your resources, or a poorly planned record session. Try defragging the hard drive before you record discs, and if the defrag utility keeps restarting, it's usually a sign that some other task is competing with it for the hard drive's attention. If you're running on battery, try recording with the AC adapter plugged in, as the battery may not be able to continually source sufficient power to get through a recording cycle.

Sole task? Close all other tasks so that the recording process is the only job your laptop is working on. Get offline, turning off your wireless connection or unplugging your connection to the high speed modem or router. Other tasks can include work you are doing in another program, as well as background tasks, like virus shield programs and fax/phone software. There are various 3rd party software packages capable of controlling background tasks, but you can usually get by with Crtl-Alt-Del and the Windows Task List, once you get a feel for which tasks are superfluous to what you're doing. If the recording process won't go through even at slow speed, it's possible that all of the media you've tried writing is either bad or not suited for the recorder you are using. Otherwise, the failure is likely due to the hardware. The recording laser may have failed or may not be generating enough power (you can try cleaning the lens) or the speed regulation for the drive may poor. As long as it reads discs correctly, it's much cheaper and simpler to replace it with an external USB burner than to replace the internal drive for what may still turn out to be an esoteric software problem.

Disc play in other drives? Does the disc record properly, read or play fine in the drive you recorded it in, but fail to play in other computer drives or in consumer devices, such as stereos and DVD players? The rewriteable media often fails completely in read-only drives, like standard CD ROM drives or DVD set-top boxes. Check with the manufacturer's specifications for the target device, the device you want to read the recorded disc in, to make sure you are using a compatible media and format. There are a sickening number of official formats and variations for recordable CDs and DVDs and many of them aren't supported by commercial playback devices, and never will be. The rule of thumb for recording data discs that will be readable in the maximum number of other computers is to use the write-once, CDR or DVD-R media.

Music CDs that you want to play in a stereo must be recorded on CDR, not CDRW, and the burner software must be set to record them in the CD-DA (Redbook) format. Writing a bunch of .wav files to a CD, even at the proper sampling frequency and in stereo, will not result in a CD that's playable in a stereo. It's the format that counts. You don't have to buy the more expensive CDR blanks labeled "CD Audio" blanks or the like, these are only required for dedicated (non PC connected) CDR devices. DVD players usually support multiple media types, but you need to check the documentation for the final word.

Troubleshooting Sound

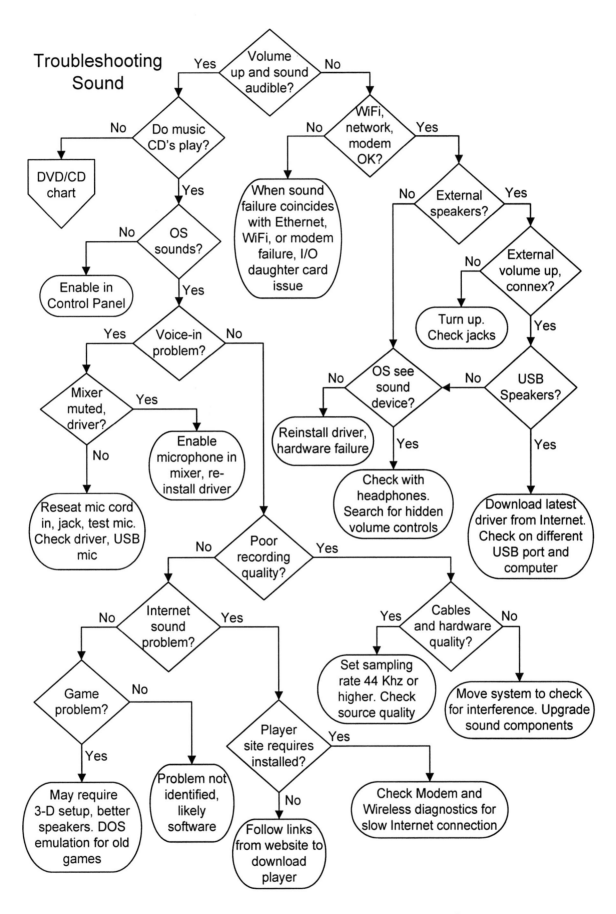

Volume up and sound audible?
- Yes → **Do music CD's play?**
  - No → DVD/CD chart
  - Yes → **OS sounds?**
    - No → Enable in Control Panel
    - Yes → **Voice-in problem?**
      - Yes → **Mixer muted, driver?**
        - Yes → Enable microphone in mixer, re-install driver
        - No → Reseat mic cord in, jack, test mic. Check driver, USB mic
      - No → **Poor recording quality?**
        - No → **Internet sound problem?**
          - No → **Game problem?**
            - Yes → May require 3-D setup, better speakers. DOS emulation for old games
            - No → Problem not identified, likely software
          - Yes → **Player site requires installed?**
            - Yes → Check Modem and Wireless diagnostics for slow Internet connection
            - No → Follow links from website to download player
        - Yes → **Cables and hardware quality?**
          - Yes → Set sampling rate 44 Khz or higher. Check source quality
          - No → Move system to check for interference. Upgrade sound components
- No → **WiFi, network, modem OK?**
  - No → When sound failure coincides with Ethernet, WiFi, or modem failure, I/O daughter card issue
  - Yes → **External speakers?**
    - No → **OS see sound device?**
      - No → Reinstall driver, hardware failure
      - Yes → Check with headphones. Search for hidden volume controls
    - Yes → **External volume up, connex?**
      - No → Turn up. Check jacks
      - Yes → **USB Speakers?**
        - No → **OS see sound device?**
        - Yes → Download latest driver from Internet. Check on different USB port and computer

167

Troubleshooting Sound

168

Volume up and sound audible? Check any external volume controls first, usually on the side or front edge of the laptop. We'll come back to the volume being up again, but if you aren't getting audible sound out of your laptop, the first thing to check that the sound isn't muted by a checkbox on the volume control and that the slider isn't all the way at the bottom. The basic volume control is normally present in the system tray at the bottom right of the screen, with a little speaker as the icon. If you can't see it on a Windows system, try expanding the tray menu by clicking the left arrow in the tray, and be patient if the laptop is still booting. You can always get to the basic volume control through Windows Control Panel, and you can also change the settings there to add the control to the system tray.

WiFi, network, modem OK? Many laptop manufacturers combine all of the I/O functions on a separate daughter card that rides on the motherboard. The daughter card usually includes the WiFi transceiver, the 100/1000BaseT Ethernet adapter and the dial-up modem, along with the sound system hardware. If you lose any of these capabilities at the same time that you lose your sound, odds are the daughter card has backed out of the connector to the motherboard or simply failed. Do your research on the Internet to establish that your laptop really does have an I/O daughter card before breaking the laptop open. Make sure you find a photo illustrated guide for replacing your model's daughter card online if the manufacturer doesn't provide a manual.

External speakers? The volume control on speakers usually serves as an on/off as well. Some speakers may be powered by batteries rather than a transformer or USB connection, so double check that you don't have speakers with dead batteries. If the speakers aren't connected to the laptop by a USB port, they aren't drawing amplification power from the laptop and must be getting it from a transformer or batteries.

If your speakers are connected through a standard stereo jack, you can plug in a simple headphone to see if any sound is coming out of the jack, just don't have them on your head in case the sound is too loud. If you are using external speakers from choice rather than necessity, disconnect the external speakers and try troubleshooting with the built-in laptop speakers first. Speakers that connect directly to a stereo jack on the laptop (little circular port) are running on the built-in sound card. Speakers connected through just the USB port or through a PC card are running on their own sound device.

External volume up, connex? Laptops come equipped with an external volume control, which is handy for turning the volume up or down without having to stop what you are doing and access the control in Windows. On newer laptops, this control may be digital and integrated with the software volume, so the two don't contradict each other. But some laptops used a hardwired volume dial that can turn the sound completely off, independently of the software setting. If the dial is off, nothing you do in software will induce the laptop to produce sound. It's also a good time to check that the speaker stereo jack or USB connection is firmly in place.

USB speakers? Make sure you have the latest driver for your operating system version downloaded from the Internet and installed. Remember that USB speakers are really combining a simple USB sound card and speakers, so the software is critical. If the Windows Device Manager doesn't report any problem with the USB sound driver, everything is connected properly, all the volume controls in software and hardware are up and not muted, and you still can't get sound, either the USB port or the USB speakers are bad. Try them on another USB port and another computer before giving up on them.

OS see sound device? If the operating system doesn't see the built-in sound device, you can try reinstalling the latest driver, but unless the original driver was corrupted, it's unlikely the problem. If Device Manager reports a hardware problem, odds are the built-in sound has failed. Unless the sound functionality is on an independent daughter card in the laptop, as determined from your owner's manual or a little Internet research on your exact model, don't even think about replacing it. The cost effective solution is to add USB speakers or a more complex USB or PC card sound device to the laptop.

If you can't get sound through the internal laptop speakers, plug in external headphones just to make sure that the speaker wires inside the laptop haven't broken. This problem is more common with laptops that feature the speakers in the lid, under or alongside the screen. But software controls remain the #1 problem for laptop sound problems. Aside from the primary volume control often found in your system tray, there may be various other mixer panels and volume adjustments offered in other applications using sound. One of these can cause a complete absence of sound if the "mute" box is checked.

Do music CDs play? Does your sound system work properly with everything except music CDs? If you do have USB speakers, your DVD/CD player and your laptop motherboard must support Digital Audio Extraction (DAE) for the digital stream to be fed to the speakers. Without DAE, music CDs are not digitally processed by the laptop, only amplified. So if you have an older laptop and the sound card functions for everything except for music CDs, the problem is related to the player, not to the sound system. Check under the properties tab for the DVD/CD player and change the setting for "Enable digital CD audio" as a test. One hint that CDs are being played digitally is that the CD drive may spin up and down while playing music, rather than staying spun up at it's slowest and quietest speed. Some people disable digital CD audio for that reason, if the laptop supports the old fashioned hard wired CD connection as well.

OS sounds? In Windows, the basic "Sounds" menu is found in Control Panel. Sound events that have little speakers next to them are enabled. Enable sounds for some actions that you recognize (like "exit program" or "minimize") and see if your speakers work now. Note that Windows sounds don't need to be enabled for music CDs, videos, Internet phone or radio or games to be heard. We're just working through the possible problems by process of elimination.

Voice-in problem? Is your problem with the microphone? Check that you have the mic in the proper port. If you are doing speech recognition, you should purchase a quality noise cancellation mic, and go through the calibration and testing procedures your software will support. If you still have a sound quality problem, you may need to bypass your built-in sound card with a USB microphone or plug in PC card sound.

Mixer muted, driver? Make sure that the microphone isn't muted in the software mixer panel. Check Device Manager for any problems, and if there are any warnings ("!", "?", "i") next to the sound card, reinstall the driver. If the mute box is unchecked and there isn't a driver problem, try the microphone on another audio device and replace it if it's bad. The female audio connector or jack for the mic in laptops can easily get broken or

deformed if the microphone cord gets pulled on or kicked, and likewise, the conductors in the cord can be frayed or broken.

Poor recording quality? If your recordings sound poor when you play them back, check your patch cables and jacks for loose connections. Some cables are extremely low quality, so if you plan to do a lot of audio work, start by getting a good set. Make sure that your mixer settings (the software mixer panel) aren't uneven, muting the channels you want, or simply running an unexpected mix. Try muting any channels that aren't contributing to the recording, since they may be introducing white noise. For example, if you're recording sound from the CD, mute the mic. Don't neglect to check the quality of the audio source - if you're trying to record from a hissing tape or a scratchy recording, the sound card does not automatically filter out the unwanted noise. High end recording software does give you the option to clean up recordings, but usually after the recording process is complete.

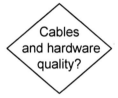

Cables and hardware quality? Laptops aren't marketed for their ability to do studio quality sound recording, and there's a reason for that. For music recording, make sure the sampling rate is set to 44 KHz, audio CD quality. Interference is always a possibility, especially if it takes the form of loud ticking or hum. Try moving the system to another location if you're recording near any electrical motors or other possible sources of low frequency interference. True audiophiles spend hundreds of dollars (or more) on audio patch cables that could be worn as jewelry, given the rare metals the wiring is drawn from. They also spend hundreds of dollars on replacement USB or plug in PC sound cards for their laptops, and although these are marketed more for their playback rather than recording quality, you get what you pay for.

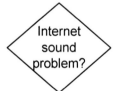

Internet sound problem? Is your problem related to playing Internet radio or other web based audio applications? If the quality stinks, it's probably your connection to the Internet. If you have a broadband (cable, DSL) connection and the quality still stinks, it could be the ISP or website is overloaded, so try again later on. It could also be that you're running too many tasks at the same time or the hard drive is near full and virtual memory is thrashing it. Check the hard drive and motherboard diagnostics for potential performance issues.

Player site requires installed? Most Internet audio applications use a third party player, such as Real Audio. These players may or may not come preinstalled on your notebook, depending on the manufacturer. If you get no Internet sound at all, but all other audio applications work, either your OS and the player software aren't getting along or you're missing a required CODEC. Try reinstalling the latest version of the software used on the particular website or research the problem on Google for your specific setup. Websites with audio content usually link to the player site from which you can download a free copy of the player, though you may have to register and reboot when it's done downloading.

Game problem? There are a number of reasons the sound quality on your system may not match your experience on somebody else's laptop. The sound card or motherboard audio in your laptop may be lower quality. The same goes for the speakers, whether internal or external. You could also be picking up interference on the speaker wires, so try routing them away from the AC power adapter and any peripheral device transformers. Laptop gaming sound will never compare well with PC gaming sound unless you've purchased a USB or PC card external sound adapter that supports 5.1 or 7.1 surround sound and scattering the required speakers around the room.

Is the audio problem with an older game? Very old games require obsolete sound card compatibility. The default settings of IRQ=5, Address=220, DMA=5 are usually required, since the game communicated directly with the sound card. You may be able to force your sound card to these settings, or, when supported by the driver, you might get by with emulating them under the sound card setup in Device Manager. There's also the possibility, if your game actually exits and runs in DOS mode, that you need to have the proper drivers installed in the DOS Startup files, config.sys and autoexec.bat. This won't be possible at all in newer Windows versions without a full DOS emulator installed.

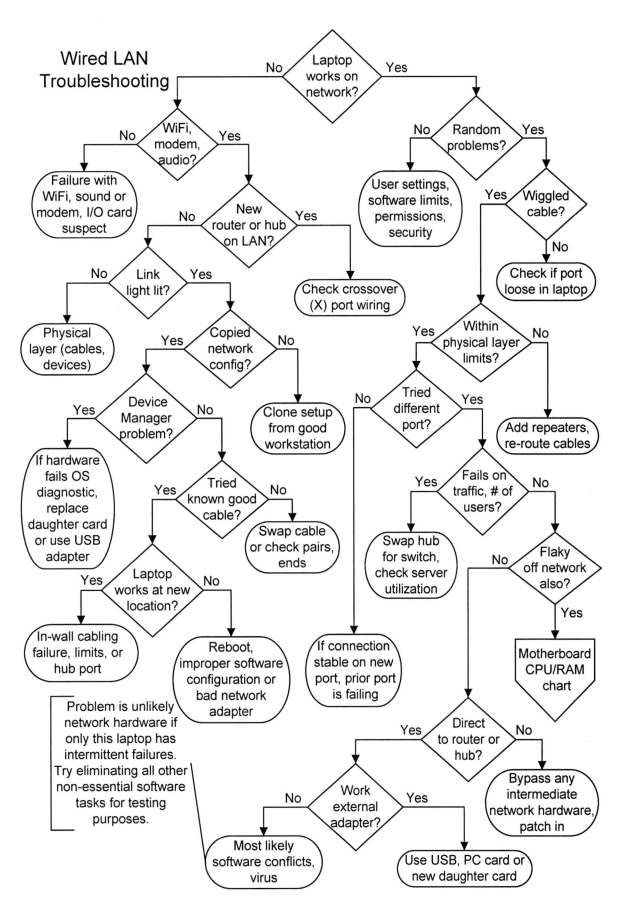

Wired LAN Troubleshooting

Laptop works on network?
- No → **WiFi, modem, audio?**
  - No → Failure with WiFi, sound or modem, I/O card suspect
  - Yes → **New router or hub on LAN?**
    - No → **Link light lit?**
      - No → Physical layer (cables, devices)
      - Yes → **Copied network config?**
        - Yes → **Device Manager problem?**
          - Yes → If hardware fails OS diagnostic, replace daughter card or use USB adapter
          - No → **Tried known good cable?**
            - Yes → **Laptop works at new location?**
              - Yes → In-wall cabling failure, limits, or hub port
              - No → Reboot, improper software configuration or bad network adapter
            - No → Swap cable or check pairs, ends
        - No → Clone setup from good workstation
    - Yes → Check crossover (X) port wiring
- Yes → **Random problems?**
  - No → User settings, software limits, permissions, security
  - Yes → **Wiggled cable?**
    - Yes → **Within physical layer limits?**
    - No → Check if port loose in laptop

Within physical layer limits?
- Yes → **Tried different port?**
  - No → If connection stable on new port, prior port is failing
  - Yes → **Fails on traffic, # of users?**
    - Yes → Swap hub for switch, check server utilization
    - No → **Direct to router or hub?**
      - Yes → **Work external adapter?**
        - No → Most likely software conflicts, virus
        - Yes → Use USB, PC card or new daughter card
      - No → Bypass any intermediate network hardware, patch in
- No → Add repeaters, re-route cables

Flaky off network also?
- No → (to Direct to router or hub?)
- Yes → Motherboard CPU/RAM chart

Problem is unlikely network hardware if only this laptop has intermittent failures. Try eliminating all other non-essential software tasks for testing purposes.

175

Laptop works on network? The laptop troubleshooting procedures on the chart are pretty evenly divided between the failure to get on the network (to the left) and the failure to stay on the network (to the right). If the laptop can access any network resources, servers, other workstations when the networking cable with the RJ-45 connector is installed, it's getting on the network. Note that some versions of Windows networking software display "remembered" resources, even when the laptop can't access them, so you'll need to click on a given resource and refresh to see if it's really available. If your laptop gets on the network and stays on the network without any glitches, but you can't access certain resources or applications, the problem is with your software settings, permissions, group memberships or security.

WiFi, modem, audio? If you lose your dial-up modem, integrated sound, or the ability to connect to a public WiFi network at the same time as you lose your wired Ethernet functionality, the problem almost certainly lies with a communications or I/O daughter board. Check the laptop manufacturer's documentation or research on the Internet before tearing the laptop apart to reseat the daughter board, inspect it for damage, or replace it if necessary. Somebody tripping over a cord or trying to walk off with the laptop still cabled to the network or the telephone jack can damage the daughter board or the motherboard connector if the ports are mounted on the board edge.

New router or hub on LAN? Is the laptop the first workstation on a new router or hub, being stacked or chained to existing hub(s) in an office network? When connecting hubs or switches with twisted pair (RJ-45 connector) cabling, whether 10BaseT , 100BaseT or Gigabyte (1000BaseT), make sure that you either connect to an "X" port (uplink port), or use a special crossover cable. A crossover cable, unlike a straight through cable, connects pins 1 and 2 on one end to 3 and 6 on the other end and vice versa for 10BaseT and 100BaseT, and also connects pins 4 and 5 with 7 and 8 on the other end and vice versa for 1000BaseT. When building crossover cables, you must use a twisted pair for each named pair for noise protection. If you do have an X or uplink port, you normally see that it is connected to an adjacent port by a line or other symbol. You can only use one or the other, since they are using the same physical circuitry, with the X port making the pair reversal. Bad hubs and routers

or bad ports on hubs and routers are as common as bad network adapters. Routers and hubs also have a power transformer that needs to be plugged into a live outlet.

Link light lit? Most laptops have LEDs right next to the RJ-45 port to show the status of the link and network activity (traffic). Green is good for a link, a blinking LED next to it indicates traffic. No link light indicates there's a break in your physical layer. Check the physical connectors at all points on your network in the failed path, and make sure that you are within all of the limits for your physical layer in terms of number of workstations and distances. Swap the laptop's networking cable to another port on the router or hub and see if it works.

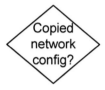

Copied network config? If all you're trying to do is connect directly to a high speed Internet router in your home, the software supplied by the phone or cable company should take care of any networking settings for you. If your laptop is the only computer getting attached to a new broadband Internet modem/router, transfer to the wireless troubleshooting flowchart and start with the "Works on Ethernet port?" symbol, following the "No" outcome.

If you're trying to connect to an office network, clone the software configuration from another workstation on the network (everything but the unique portion of the IP address, if you're set up for TCP/IP). It's easy to make a mistake with which protocol should be the default or with the spelling of a Workgroup, etc. At an active workstation, go through every option in the network setup and print screen every page and sub page that comes up. Keep it around for future reference when you run into networking problems with a similar workstation. If this is the first workstation on the network, or the second on a peer-to-peer, go with the defaults and make use of the operating system's built-in troubleshooter, at least in Windows versions. After making changes, go through a full reboot.

Device Manager problem? Does the Device Manager see the network adapter and report it to be working properly? If not, try reinstalling the driver and rebooting. In Windows, start by deleting the existing network adapter in Device Manager. If Windows doesn't find the adapter and reinstall a driver when you reboot, it's probably failed. Check that the CMOS settings are restored to their defaults. If the network adapter is integrated on a replaceable daughter board that you can get cheaply, it might be worth opening up the laptop, but otherwise, replace it with a USB or PC card network adapter.

Tried known good cable? Even if the link light is lit, it doesn't mean your cable is capable of carrying network traffic. An incredible number of techs make these cables wrong out of sheer laziness or ignorance. Don't say, "But it's a new cable!" Four conductors are actually used for normal implementations 10BaseT and 100BaseT, and the wiring is straight through, 1-1, 2-2, 3-3, 6-6. Pins 1 and 2 and pins 3 and 6 must each use a twisted pair, or the longer runs will fail and shorter runs will act unpredictably. Gigabit, or 1000BaseT cables, use all 4 pairs, with 4-4, 5-5 adding one pair and 7-7, 8-8 adding the other. In addition, visually inspect connectors to make sure they are solid and wired properly (shared pairs listed above). Squint into the transparent connector and try to take note of the color coding for each pin. Then go look at the other end of the cable and make sure that the color coding is the same, AND that a pair (i.e, blue, blue stripe) is used for the pair 1 and 2, 3 and 6, etc.

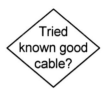

Laptop works at new location? Take the laptop to another workstation location and steal the networking cable out of that computer. If you get right on the network, that tells you that the physical link to the location where it failed is bad. That could be the patch cable, the in-wall wiring, or the port on the hub it connects to. If it doesn't work at the new location, this tells you the problem is either the network adapter or the software configuration. If there's a USB network adapter floating around the office you can try, by all means give it a shot, but the software settings are more often the culprit. Make sure the driver is up-to-date and the correct version for the OS, make sure that you have cloned all the settings (except the machine name or final IP address) from a working machine, and try going through the OS troubleshooting steps.

Random problems? Are your network access problems of a random or intermittent nature? Check for loose connectors. It's very easy to install a RJ-45 connector improperly or fail to crimp it tightly enough to hold to the cable such that it loosens up with just a minor physical movement. The problem might also be interference somewhere in the cable run. Make sure the cable isn't running directly over your ham radio set or other strong RF emitters. You could be experiencing software conflicts with other processes on the laptop. You can try eliminating all tasks except the minimal network configuration and do some large file movements to see if the hardware layer is solid. In an office environment, occasional problems are often due to loading of the network, a traffic jam.

Wiggled cable? Try wiggling the network cable very close to the laptop port while keeping an eye on the link LED. If the link LED winks when you're moving the cable and is steady otherwise (make sure you don't mistake a traffic LED for a link LED as the traffic LED's are always winking), either the connector on the cable end or the port in the laptop has a loose connection. If you're lucky, it's the cable. If not, you can try to resolder the RJ-45 connector inside the laptop if you know what you're doing, but it's safer to just buy a USB network adapter and use that instead. The killer for networking ports on laptops is when the user forgets the cable is connected and tries to walk away with the laptop.

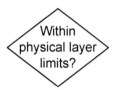

Within physical layer limits? Are you within the physical layer limits for your network? This applies to both wired and wireless networks. Don't go by the number in the IEEE standard, use the limit in the router, hub, switch or repeater documentation. Be aware that the distance limitations are based on a normal operating environment with the proper cabling or antennas installed. If your cables are made wrong, routed poorly, or are low quality, the limits will be reduced. Rerouting cables, adding repeaters (amplifiers) or eliminating sources of interference can increase the reach of your network.

Tried different port? There's no rule that says router and hub ports should have to fail all at same time, so try a different port, even if you have to disconnect somebody else for a minute. It could also be that the cable end plugged into the hub wasn't crimped on as tightly as it could have been, causing the performance of the link to be dependent on the exact position of the cable, an unacceptable situation.

Fails on traffic, # of users? Does the problem, be it lost connections, slow performance or anything else, occur during periods when network traffic is high or a large number of users are logged on? There are many reasons a network can bog down or have trouble in high traffic or high user count situations, including the natural limitations of the technologies being used.

In general, if you are using a passive hub in a business or educational environment, you can greatly increase your network performance during high traffic periods by swapping the hub for an active switch. Also, if you are running a hybrid LAN, with a mix of 10BaseT and 100BaseT and 1000BaseT adapters, you should think about upgrading them all to 1000BaseT, providing the cable plant is all Cat 5 and you haven't scavenged the previously unused pairs for some kludge.

Flaky off network also? If your laptop suffers from random lock-ups, data corruption or poor performance when you aren't connected to the network, you've started troubleshooting in the wrong place. Start with motherboard, CPU and RAM failure if the problem is lock-ups, but you should follow through the overheating and hard drive troubleshooting flowcharts as well.

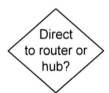

Direct to router or hub? If you're in a home or small business networking environment, bypass any repeaters and hubs and don't use a port replicator or docking station until you solve the problem. In a larger networking environment, you might try sneaking the laptop into the wiring closet and patching it directly into the hub with a short cable if all else fails. Check for physical cable damage on your patch cable. The sheathing on the Cat 5 cables is thin and the inner conductors can be easily broken if the cable is stretched or crimped.

Work external adapter? If bypassing the laptop's built-in networking adapter with a USB or PC card networking adapter cures the random drops, just keep using the replacement adapter. If it doesn't cure the problem, either you have some other hardware issue that only manifests itself when you're running certain networking tasks, or the problem is of the malware/software corruption variety.

Keyboard, Pointer and USB

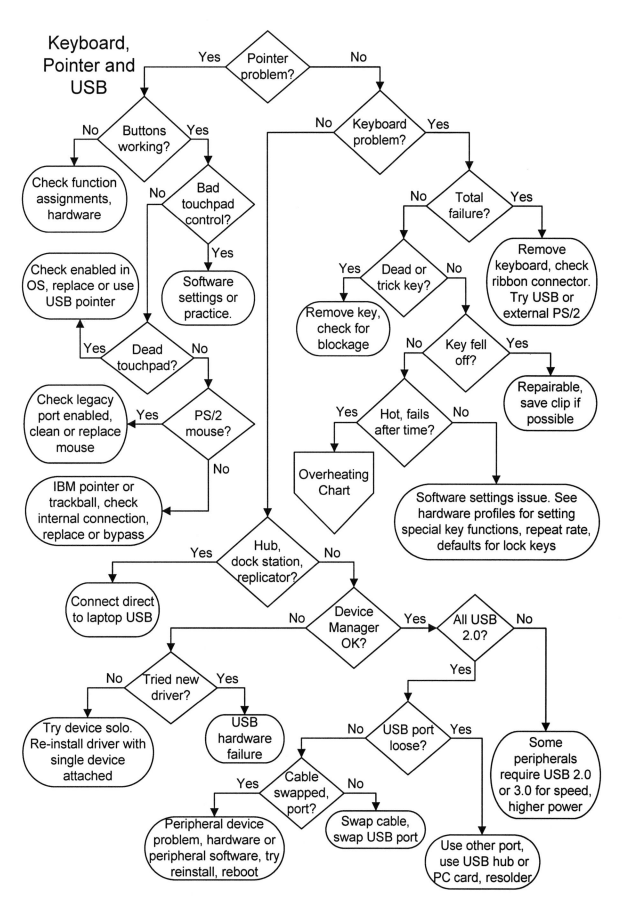

183

Keyboard, Pointer and USB

Pointer problem? Is the problem with your touchpad, IBM style pointer, trackball, mouse or graphics tablet? The touchpad is the pointing device for the vast majority of laptops being sold today. If your problem is with the keyboard, any USB devices or peripherals, continue to the right.

Buttons working? Do the buttons for your touchpad, on your mouse, or in the palm rest area if you have an IBM style keyboard pointer, select or activate the text or controls on screen? If neither button works, either the software assignments for the button actions are set to do something other than you assume, or there's a hardware problem. Find the controls for the button functions for your pointer, usually accessed through a system tray icon in Windows and always available through Control Panel. If the buttons are enabled and set to do the normal functions, shut down and check CMOS Setup on reboot to make sure they aren't disabled there. If everything is correct in software and they don't work, it's likely that the cable to the touchpad or pointer has come undone and you'll have to remove the keyboard if you want to check it. Alternatively, you can switch to a USB pointing device, like a mouse or tablet.

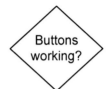

If one button works and the other doesn't, try reversing the assignments for the buttons, changing from left-handed to right-handed, and see if the functioning button changes. If it does, the problem is that the software assignments for the button that doesn't work simply don't match the action you thought it would. However, if the functioning button doesn't change, it's a genuine hardware failure of that button, which you'd have to replace if you really need it and don't want to work with a USB replacement pointer or mouse.

Bad touchpad control? Nearly all problems with controlling the pointer through the touchpad are due to the software settings. If you keep launching applications you don't intend to when trying to move the pointer on screen, or if you get crazy scrolling or system prompts for actions you aren't trying to carry out, odds are the touchpad is set up for various shortcuts. Touchpads offer a serious array of shortcuts through touching the corners of the pad, moving your finger along the side, tapping, any specially recognized action the programmers could think of. You can turn off all these enhanced functions in the touchpad controls so it does nothing but move the screen pointer along with your fingertip, or you can familiarize yourself with the controls that appear useful and keep them.

Dead touchpad? If you get no action at all from the touchpad, the first thing to do is to plug in a USB mouse so you can navigate through the operating system without having to resort to the <Tab>, spacebar and arrow keys. Check the touchpad properties in Windows, first making sure that it is enabled, and then checking the hardware profile to see if Windows reports that it is operating properly. If Windows sees a problem, power down and restart the laptop, then enter CMOS Setup and make sure the touchpad hasn't been disabled. Finally, check the manufacturer's website to see if an updated driver is available. If everything is as correct as you can make it in software, it's possible that the touchpad itself has failed or the connector has worked loose thanks to all the vibrations from typing. If you can find a good illustrated guide specific to your model for removing the keyboard and gaining access to the touchpad, you can check the connections and decide if you want to try replacing it.

PS/2 mouse? We're including any type of mouse port mouse here, one that plugs into a little circular port which is normally green, as opposed to USB. If the pointer doesn't move on screen and the buttons don't work, check the connection and make sure it's enabled in CMOS Setup. If it still does nothing, try another mouse. If the pointer works in one direction only, horizontal or vertical, the mouse just needs the lint cleaned off the little roller bars inside. If the buttons don't work, check the software assignments for the buttons, and if they are correct, replace the mouse.

If you have an IBM style pointer or a trackball and you're having problems with the buttons, go back up to the first decision diamond in this tree and read the troubleshooting for the "No" answer to "Buttons clicking?" If the little foam cover on the pointer is loose, you can get a bag full of replacements online. If the pointer wanders off in one direction when you're not touching it, check if there's a recalibration option included with the pointer software. If not, you can try over working it in the opposite direction to see if it was just a little sprung, but it is a failure mode with pointers and joysticks, and it may have to be replaced.

Keyboard problem? The diagnostic path to the right is for problems with built-in laptop keyboard. Any problems with an externally attached keyboard, continue down to USB troubleshooting, or if it's a PS/2 keyboard, replace the thing for a couple bucks!

Total failure? Is the keyboard completely useless, to the point that you can't even access CMOS Setup before the operating system launches? The first thing to do is to try a cheap external USB keyboard, just to find out if the problem is really your integrated keyboard, or a laptop that is ignoring all user input. If the laptop boots and the touchpad still works to navigate in the operating system, either the keyboard connector has vibrated off the motherboard, or you have a hardware failure. Since traveling with an extra keyboard defeats the point of owning a laptop for many people, it's worth finding a good photo illustrated guide online to replacing the keyboard for your exact model, opening up the laptop and redoing the keyboard connector. At that time, you can decide if you want to gamble on a replacement keyboard membrane if redoing the connector doesn't work. If an external PS/2 keyboard works on the special keyboard port, the keyboard controller on the motherboard is good, but if only a USB keyboard works, a replacement membrane is a real gamble.

Dead or trick key? Does a single key malfunction on a regular basis, or all of the time? If it's gotten to the point that you can't work with the integrated keyboard and always use a detached USB or PS/2 keyboard, you have nothing to lose in prying off the key and checking if it's gunked up by hair, food crumbs or anonymous gudge. Using a butter knife or a fine pair of needle nose pliers, you should be able to unhook the plastic clip from the key once you pry it up a little, rather than tearing it off and hoping for the best. If the clip was being interfered with, the key will work fine when you replace it. It's an excruciatingly frustrated job for the uninitiated because it involves working blindly to re-catch the clip inside the key. If the key behavior doesn't change, the failure is in the domed membrane contact, and the only cure is to replace the whole membrane, which you buy (thankfully) with the keys attached. If you aren't a touch typer, you can download a software key remapper, which allows you to change the functionality of keys. That way, if you've lost your "A" key, you can change one of the top Function or special Windows keys into the new "A" for when you use the laptop on the road.

Key fell off? A couple of the larger keys, including the space bar, and sometimes the <shift> keys, <enter> and <backspace>, can use metal wire spring clips. These aren't as hard to replace as individual keys, and you may even find them for sale individually if you spend enough time searching the web for parts for your exact model. All of the other keys are retained by small plastic clips that hold the keys by inserting the clip ends in tiny holes or channels under the key. There's very little spring force involved, the plastic has just enough strength to keep the clip ends engaged with the key.

Sometimes a key falls off because a little foreign matter has gotten underneath and eventually worked its way into the hole or channel, releasing the end of the clip. The clip will be undamaged, you just have to clean out the key, study the latching mechanism to figure out how it's supposed to go on, and replace the key with a great deal of patience. However, if a key is ripped off the keyboard and the plastic clip is damaged, the odds of getting the key back on in a working state are much reduced. Your best bet, rather than shopping for a replacement clip, is shopping for a junk laptop from the same model family. If you find one cheap, you can decide between trying to swap keyboards (the junk laptop keyboard may have its own problems), or scavenging a clip from it. You can also download a software keyboard remapper as mentioned in the dead key troubleshooting.

Hot, fails after time? The keyboard itself shouldn't generate any heat, so the problem is due to overheating below the keyboard that's coming right through. Since the keyboard takes up the majority of the top surface area of the laptop, it's not that uncommon of a problem. You should start by researching complaints about overheating with your model on the Internet to see if it's a "normal" problem and if there are any trick solutions. Otherwise, see the troubleshooting flowchart for overheating.

If you're getting extra characters while you type, yet the key isn't physically sticking (what we'd call a trick key), the problem is often in software, with the typomatic repeat control. You can try changing the repeat rate settings for the keyboard in Windows Control Panel, and sometimes there's a hardware control in CMOS Setup as well. But if it only happens with one key, and cleaning doesn't help, it could be the membrane is faulty or just

188

worn out. But try an external keyboard before jumping to conclusions, just to make sure it isn't a software setting.

Hub, dock station, replicator? Is the USB device you are having trouble with plugged in through a USB hub, a docking station or a port replicator? If so, connect it directly to a USB port on the laptop and if it still doesn't work, continue the troubleshooting process to the right. If your USB ports on the laptop work fine, but your powered USB hub, docking station or port replicator doesn't work, you may be dealing with bad hardware, or the software may not be functioning properly. If the device is plug-n-play, and the operating system doesn't require any third-party software to be installed for it to operate, than the hardware itself is probably at fault. If it does require software drivers, make sure you've downloaded the latest version from the manufacturer of the device on the Internet.

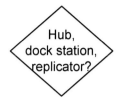

Device Manager OK? Windows Device Manager will list all of the USB hardware the laptop recognizes, host controllers and root hubs. Make sure to disconnect any external USB devices before checking. Make sure that USB is enabled in CMOS Setup. If there is a warning symbol, when you click on that USB device, you may still see the message "This device is working properly", but go through the Windows troubleshooting anyway. Either the driver software is corrupted or there's a problem with the hardware. In the advanced properties for the USB port in Windows Device Manager, there may be an option to rollback the driver to a previous version. This is always worth trying, especially if the USB port stopped working after an automated Windows update.

Tried new driver? You can try to delete the USB device in Device Manager, shut down the laptop, and Windows should re-detect it and install the driver again when the laptop reboots. If you did locate a new driver for the USB ports on the manufacturer's website and it didn't correct the Device Manager error, the motherboard USB has likely failed. If the ports are reported healthy in Device Manager until you connect an external USB device, that external device must be bad.

As long as one USB port still works, you can use an inexpensive external USB hub to attach multiple USB peripherals. You can also purchase one of those poorly named PC cards for your laptop that will host a number of USB ports that bypass the motherboard USB entirely.

All USB 2.0? Many newer peripherals require USB 2.0 to function, especially high speed devices like external hard drives and DVD recorders. While most USB devices can still operate in a backwards compatible mode with USB 1.1, this functionality will slowly go away as USB 1.1 ports disappear with obsolete computers. USB 3.0 is just pushing into the market, but USB 3.0 devices should remain backward compatible with USB 2.0 for a long time to come.

Some laptops came with a mix of USB 2.0 and USB 1.1 ports. If you are having trouble with a high speed USB device, make sure you are using it on a USB 2.0 port, and if you aren't sure all of your ports are 2.0 or which is which, just try the device on the other ports. If you are getting write errors with an external hard drive, or any time-out related errors with any USB device that works intermittently, make sure that power management isn't cutting the USB power to the port. The USB Root Hubs in Device Manager have a Power Management option, the default setting for which in Windows is to allow Windows to turn off the port to save power. Try changing the setting.

USB port loose? If the USB port feels loose in the laptop and you are having problems with the devices connected, you should stop using it. The solder connections may have broken or the port itself may have been bent or the metal distorted from somebody yanking or tripping over an attached USB cord. If you have advanced soldering skills and you really need the port, you can dissemble the laptop to resolder or replace it. But there are so many other options, from adding an external USB hub on a working USB port, to a docking station, port replicator or PC card solution, that trying to fix the physical failure of a port isn't usually necessary.

Cable swapped, port? USB cables, like all cables, come in a variety of qualities. The USB scheme is very simple, the four conductor cable includes a signaling pair (the serial bus), a power supply and a ground. But a poorly made cable or one made for a USB device you purchased ten years ago and found in a drawer may not be up to working with a high speed drive, printer, etc. Never give up on a USB peripheral without trying it with a USB cable rated for the speed of the device, ie, USB 2.0 or

USB 3.0 (also called High Speed). You should always try the peripheral not only on multiple USB ports as well, but on another laptop or PC with working USB ports.

USB is very solid technology, and the majority of the problems you'll have with USB peripherals are with the software that does or doesn't accompany them. Many USB devices are plug-n-play with the newer versions of Windows, but that doesn't mean they will work with older versions of Windows without a special driver download, if at all. You may also have to install special drivers for your Linux or Mac OS system. Also, pay attention to any error conditions displayed with LED's on your USB peripherals. You don't want to call in a technician or start replacing hardware when the problem is a printer paper jam, a dead inkjet cartridge, or an external drive with a failed transformer.

LaVergne, TN USA
29 July 2010
191283LV00002B/8/P

9 780972 380157